D1527255

TANTUM FORTIS DEBEAT PARERE

death by children

I HAD KIDS SO YOU DON'T HAVE TO

By
Bull Garlington

First Edition

EVERYTHING GOES MEDIA

Chicago • Milwaukee
www.everythinggoesmedia.com

Death by Children: I Had Kids So You Don't Have To
Christopher "Bull" Garlington

Published October 2013 by:
Everything Goes Media
www.everythinggoesmedia.com

Publisher's Cataloging-In-Publication Data
(Prepared by The Donohue Group, Inc.)

Garlington, Christopher.
   Death by children : I had kids so you don't have to / Christopher "Bull" Garlington. – 1st ed.

   p. : ill. ; cm.

   Issued also as an ebook.
   ISBN: 978-1-893121-99-7

   1. Parenthood—Humor. 2. Parent and child—Humor. 3. Child rearing—Humor. 4. American wit and humor. 5. Essays. I. Title.

PS3607.A75 A6 2013
818/.6   2013939510

   18 17 16 15 14 13   10 9 8 7 6 5 4 3 2 1

Interior and Cover Design: Mike Wykowski
Drawings: Sarah Garlington

To my family: [My Attorney] [1], Rah, and Roon

[1] [My Attorney] refers to the woman I married, who, in the interest
of her career, forbids me to publish her actual name which is not
[My Attorney] Garlington. *Oh, crap*.

CONTENTS

THE DOGS

THE HORROR

MY STUPID CHILDHOOD

THE DAD

INTRODUCTION

I am a terrible parent. I'm not fishing for compliments here–
I really am unqualified for the job. I am lazy, indifferent, hard to
impress, and generally trying to worm my way out of whatever
pressing responsibility my kids require.

I think Dr. Spock is an idiot. I think the Tiger Mom is insane.
I think Dr. Phil owes more to his mustache and his pedantic
delivery than any actual wisdom about being a dad. Here's the

naked, terrifying truth about parenting: None of us know what we're doing. Ever.

I know I don't. After twenty years of it, I can safely report my kids raised themselves. I subscribed to the parenting style of calculated neglect. Unless one of my kids was bleeding or on fire, I saw no real reason to get off the couch. It sounds horrible but they've come out swinging as they plunge into adulthood. They are marvelous, gifted, witty, and a pleasure to live with. And I'm pretty sure I had nothing to do with it.

Still, there are times when I have to explain myself (to cops, church wardens, and angry neighbors) and for those times, I present my manifesto of things I will not, anymore, do.

I Will Not...

1. I will not insert Bigfoot or flying saucers into my readings from the Bible just to make it "more interesting."

2. I will not teach my son that mooning is considered a polite greeting in Papua New Guinea.

3. I will not teach my son that burping aloud is OK if you turn it into a word.

4. I will not consistently offer that the sound of my own fart was actually that of a rare "barking spider."

5. I will not fart on my son.

6. I will not teach my son the ancient rubric, "Why fart and waste it, when you can burp and taste it."

7. Apparently it is NOT OK for him to have a Mohawk when he attends a private, upscale Catholic school.

8. Peanut butter and Hershey's chocolate milk mix is not an acceptable substitute for a healthy sandwich.

9. I will not teach my son to forgive the fat bully kid on his basketball team for being such a dickwad by patting him on the shoulder and saying, "It's OK, being adopted must be hard."

10. I will not laugh uncontrollably when my son shoots himself in the finger, point blank, with the compressed air Nerf-pellet gun I told him he couldn't play with.

11. I will not tell the story about how he thought he'd lost his balls. *Anymore.*

12. I will not convince my son, over the period of one year, through subtle slips and through stories of his "difficult capture and hair removal surgery" that he started life as a monkey.

13. Or a girl.

14. I will not wait until we are deep into a forest trail to talk about how people who get pythons from pet stores secretly release them into the forest preserves when they get too big.

15. I will not—look, there is no such thing as being able to kill someone with a single touch.

16. I will not teach my daughter her best friend is a ninja "in hiding."

17. I will not persuade my children I am, "every once in a while," possessed by the devil.

18. I will not teach my children that the TV remote will work on the neighbor's set "if you try hard."

THE BOY

Every father sees himself in his son. *Except me.* My son is nothing like me. He is tall, blonde, hairless, handsome, and smart. He has blue eyes and an encyclopedic knowledge of music from 1967 forward. He is wise and cautious and knows how to match his socks.

That's now, of course. He started out as a goofball kid and there were times when I wasn't sure he'd make it out alive.

GUN CONTROL

I don't own a gun. Never have. Not because of any overt political or personal views, but for the simple reason that I am as they say down south, *afflicted*, and I would most likely use that weapon to shoot my own feet, an ineptitude I've passed to my son.

We were visiting family; it was a father and son vacation to the motherland, the red dirt state of my birth, Alabama, where sons are born with a gun in one hand and a football in the other. We arrived on my nephew's birthday. My nephew was getting a gun.

Not a *real* gun. He was buying an Airsoft pistol—it shoots tiny little plastic beads that couldn't hurt a fly. My sister loaded her van full of boys and we went to the local fake arms dealer, a sports store, where my son found himself standing before a wall of fake firearms.

"Can I have a gun? *Everyone else has one.*"

Kid logic. It seems stupid in retrospect but something about the lure of fake weaponry and the realization that without a fake gun my son would be fake unarmed alarmed me in the dark recesses of my cowboy brain. Plus, my wife wasn't there. So I got two.

Back at the party, the adults were drinking sweet iced tea in the kitchen while the boys slaughtered each other in the basement. My son showed up.

"They're shooting me!"

"Well shoot back."

"I am!"

"What's the problem?"

"They're *good!*"

"Welcome to Alabama, kid."

Ten minutes later, two cousins appeared.

"We think Roon should sit this one out."

"Why?"

"He's crazy."

"He's shooting us while we reload."

"Welcome to Chicago, kids."

I went in the basement. There was my son, eyes wild, a gun in both hands, laughing maniacally, shooting neon green plastic balls in every direction while my nephews hid behind a couch and tried to ignore him. I dragged him upstairs for a talk.

"I think it's time to put the gun away."

He waved the gun around like a drunken Nicaraguan dictator.

"Dad, it's totally saf—"

He's cut off by a loud click–the only sound these guns make–and remained silent for a split second as his eyes widened and we both looked down at his index finger, wrapped snugly over the barrel of the fake gun, a finger rapidly turning crimson. The scream came from deep within him, where it had been wrapped around his spleen, patiently waiting to deploy. Now it uncurled and filled the house with a splenetic wail of oh-my-god-I-shot-myself.

This was one of those moments where a true dad, a good dad, a Tom Hanks in the role of dad, would take a knee, soothe the boy's affliction, and teach a life lesson.

You know where this is going, right?

I fell out of my chair. I laughed so hard I almost choked. Was my son crying? Yes, yes, he was. Was it my fault? Yes. Absolutely. Entirely. Did any of that stop me from laughing? No. It. Did. Not.

Because that's a life lesson as valuable as anything Tom Hanks could offer: sometimes, you're an idiot. Being aware of one's capability for genuine stupidity is important. When my son is a man and he fantasizes about buying a gun, he'll look at his finger and remember he's an idiot and go to a bookstore.

RAISED BY GOOGLE

There are vital rites of passage fathers and sons must go through. They are the most important, unmissable milestones of a father's journey. I have experienced exactly none of them.

My wife stole one, a titanic disaster on her part, and all I'm going to tell you is he was three and it involved aiming.

All other benchmarks of tradition were ripped from my clawed, grasping fingers by my archrival, the un-father, a sinister, soulless substitute: My son was raised by Google.

It's my fault. I gave him unrestricted access to the Internet. There are parents tearing this article out of the magazine in pediatric offices all over Chicago to provide the DCFS evidence of my madness and neglect, but I tell you, the worst thing to come out of it is an affinity for highbrow knock-knock jokes and Zen Buddhism, the ability to trounce me in the recollection of arcane 70s arena rock trivia, and oh, that Google is his real father.

Take fishing. Classic dad. I took him out in the middle of a lake to teach him how to tie a hook with a secret fisherman's knot handed down through my family, an heirloom knot. I reach for his rod, employing my raspiest McQueen.

"Let me show you how to tie that hoo—"

He whips his lure out into the lake like he's on *Bass Pros*.

"I tied it on with an eight-fold Japanese blood knot."

"Who taught you that?"

"Googled it."

Later on I take a long look at the darkening sky, note the stumpy quality of the waves, and see all the locals packing it in. Years of experience have taught me these are sure signs an NFL game is on in five minutes. Awesome, I'd like to see Google teach him—

"Dad, you see how the swans are tucking their heads into their wings?"

"Birds are stupid, son."

"Aaaaactually, they know it's about to rain so hard they won't have time to make it to shore."

"That's idioti—[THUNDEROUS DOWNPOUR]. How'd you know that!?"

My son pauses as if he's taking a moment to compose a response, to level his tone so as not to insult me. Quietly, he says, "I Googled it, Dad," squinting into the distance, "I Googled it."

Google is like a greedy stepfather stealing all my thunder. Meaningful moments are shot down before I can get the words out of my mouth with "Googled it, Dad, no problem!"

Google tells him stories, it shows him cool Zippo lighter tricks, it can teach him anything through a series of simple step-by-step videos, it's never wrong, and it never sleeps. Google's a better father than I'll ever be.

But I'm not going down without a fight. I'm not entirely useless. I'd like to see Google give him a hundred bucks and a ride to Six Flags.

POISON CONTROL POSTER CHILD TRAINING

Nine-year-old boys are doomed by their curiosity. I know a lot of nine-year-old boys and they're all lucky to be alive. I thank God every day for their obsession with video games because it turns them into mindless, sedentary zombies—and keeps them off the street, away from power tools.

But sometimes it gets away from them and their curiosity makes them do something so irreversibly stupid that they lose an arm or worse. This kind of behavior is usually preceded by a question, either to themselves or a friend who is egging them on, something along the lines of, "What does this thing do?" And thwack: meet Stumpy.

So I'm at the kitchen table writing, which involves, believe it or not, an ungodly and tedious amount of staring into space, when I notice my son is examining a mint. It's one of those highly technical mints where a hard, chalky candy is welded seamlessly around a translucent gel mint. It has a demarcation that Roon has discovered and he's decided to find out what's inside the thing by prying the two halves asunder, and what he finds is that the gel, cinnamon flavored, is pressurized and the oil of cinnamon has exploded from inside the gel and taken up residence in his eye socket, which has, as I look up, welded itself shut.

But I didn't see any of that happen. Though it occurred directly across the table from me, I was writing and, so, oblivious to anything other than the fine and specialized fiction, which I labor to produce. All I saw was my son calmly holding his hands to his eyes. So I ask him, calmly, "What's the matter?"

Now, I don't get upset. I get annoyed. If a kid saws him arm off, though he may do irreversible damage to himself, the real problem is that he's ruined my day. Now I gotta do first aid, clean up the blood, do something with the arm, call 911. It's an inglorious pain in the ass and just pisses me off. And, really, most accidents and traumatic events are way overblown. Most things are of the splinter-in-the-finger varietal and should not intrude on the well-deserved quiet afternoon of an adult. So I don't go looking for problems. I don't jump up from the chair when something crashes; I don't put down my magazine right away when a kid comes in with a nosebleed; and I never, ever ask, "What's wrong?" I don't want to know. So when my wife sees me rising gently from my chair, she explodes.

I see Roon hunch a little harder and a wail unwinds from somewhere deep in his knees. It comes out of his mouth, shoots through the ceiling like a missile, and explodes over our house, shaking the roof beams and curling the floorboards up, and Roon, suddenly lost in a plume of hurt, screams:

"My eyyyyyyyyyyyyyyyyyes!"

[My Attorney] hits the dining room in full charge. She swoops Roon up, throws me the phone, and yells: "POISON CONTROL!" The way someone might yell, "GRENADE!" She pushes her son into the shower, turns his face into a full stream of ice cold water, and Clockwork Oranges his eyes wide open

13

while he screams.

Poison Control tells me we're doing the right thing, that cinnamon oil is unlikely to cause any real damage and ought to stop hurting in about fifteen minutes, and maybe I ought to try a piece of bread. So I take a piece of bread into the shower with my son still bawling, and [My Attorney] tries to stick it on his eye to sponge up the oil but it dissolves.

Roon is sobbing and yelling that he's blinded himself, asking [My Attorney] if he'll ever see again, and [My Attorney] of course runs all the scenarios through her mental actuarial tables, her ephemeris of disaster, and yells at me to ask Poison Control about it, and the woman from Poison Control is trying to reassure me and says that really, such a small amount of the material won't cause permanent damage and I can call her back in an hour and let her know how things went.

So everything gets better all of a sudden. Roon stops crying. He and [My Attorney] emerge in a heap of damp towels, fully clothed, wild haired and red eyed, and slightly addled like they just washed up from a shipwreck.

HAPPY PULASKI DAY!

[My Attorney] went to Delaware this week for a patent trial in which a lot of people grumbled and kvetched about who owns the intellectual rights to the number seven. So I'm left at home with the monkeys.

Girl monkey tells me she doesn't have school Monday. I ask why. She declares: "It's Pulaski Day!"

Boy Monkey chimes in, "Oh yeah, we don't have school either—Happy Pulaski Day!"

My kids go to different schools. Monkeyboy goes to a Catholic school and Girlmonkey goes to a public school. They're both geniuses, and the state mandated ISAT testing pretty much lends measurable evidence to the idea that they're smarter than me. This is a concept they exploit mercilessly and they've come to accept it as fact. So they assume any idea they have for putting one over on me is a perfect idea since naturally it will exceed my stated level of understanding. I firmly believe they sometimes think that when they talk in my presence I think they're speaking a different language. Their arrogance is unfathomable.

And dead on. When Monkeyboy said he had Pulaski Day off, I didn't even blink. I just thought, "Great, I can sleep in."

His school wakes me up at 8:45.

"We're just calling about Roon's absence."

"That little bastard."

"Pardon me?"

"He told me it was Pulaski Day."

"That's not a Catholic Holiday."

"I'm going to kill him."

"So he won't be coming in?"

"Oh, he'll be there." [Evil music rises . . .]

When I want to, I have a voice like a cannon. I reserve this voice for unsolicited calls from mortgage resellers and Republicans. I used *vox artilleria* to wake up Roon by loudly wishing him, "HAPPY PULASKI DAY!" He leapt straight out of the covers and landed feet first in an excuse.

"I said I *thought* we had Pulaski Day off!"

I hadn't done laundry so the only gym pants he had were a pair discarded by his sister. They were too big and sagged around his ankles like he was wearing swanky potato sacks. I almost make him walk to school, but I honestly believe it's so cold outside his brain might explode like an ice-decavitated Pepsi can.

Later: At school, he and his friend, who-just-happens-to-be-a-girl whom shall never be referred to as a girlfriend, __ __ __ __ __ __ __, have a knock-down drag-out over which dog is most popular, border collies (ours) or bulldogs (hers). Pretty soon they have the room divided and are at each other's throats like one of those weird psyche experiments from the 60s, and now he and __ __ __ __ __ __ __, his friend-who-just-happens-to-be-a-girl, aren't speaking. Which is OK because,

"Dude, she's a girl."

Later yet: To fulfill a promise, I take the kids to dinner at Gino's East where you can write on the walls. I heard they serve pizza but scribbling on the bench is the principle attraction. I stop by Walgreens and bone up with Sharpies and gel pens and we get a booth and start drawing on everything in sight. The simians disappear into the gothic depths of the restaurant, and I busy myself with some intricate graffiti. The male child comes back with the satisfied swagger of a dictionary-loving preteen who's managed to write a word on the wall so vulgar and satanic a nun would drop dead after one syllable. He also sports a dumbass badge of truly classic stature: he's used the brown Sharpie to draw a mustache on himself.

A. Sharp. Eee.

I crack up and he tries to shrug it off, but I catch him trying to read the fine print on the marker later on.

"Dude, are you aware you have a mustache?"

"Yeah!"

"Are you aware that a Sharpie is a permanent marker?"

"Yeah, uh, what?"

"You're going to have that mustache for three weeks."

"I can get it off."

"How?"

"Spit."

"Jesus Haploid Christ. Why'd you draw a mustache on yourself?"

"I didn't, Rah did."

"Well, why, what—how?!" The kids know when I'm about to explode. He cuts me off.

"Dude, I let her."

"Why?!"

"Because she bet me I wouldn't do it! Duh!"

THE ITSY BITSY ALL CONSUMING FEAR OF SPIDERS

My son is Sasquatchian. His shoes are vast displays of remarkable biodiversity. Our doorways all have an arch worn into the lintel where his head knocks the wood away. When he was a baby, we called him Bam Bam for his weird, natural, chimp-like strength, which hasn't waned in the least. He can palm a watermelon. He's strong. He's tall. He's afraid of spiders.

I worry that it's my fault. Well sort of. All kids are born with a nascent fear of the micro and multi-legged. They are genetically predisposed to run wildly away from anything squirmy and squishable because those things are poison-y. This fear diminishes by half as soon as any self-respecting kid discovers a magnifying glass or a flyswatter. They suddenly have dominion over an entire class of organisms, a dominion they gleefully demonstrate through garden-hose-ant-hill-tsunami-disaster-modeling. Only a handful of species remain on the short list of things that make kids go AAAAAAAAAAAAAAAAA and run flailing away: little spiders, regular spiders, and really, really big spiders.

My son's fear of spiders comes from his fascination with them. As soon as he could read, he shut himself up inside a chair fort in the kids' section of the library and read every book about spiders they had. I expected him to emerge with a healthy respect for and scholarly delight in our arachnidan friends.

Instead, he crawled out pale and concerned.

Dad: "What's wrong, Kiddo?"

Kiddo: "Did you know there are more spiders than people?"

Dad: "Yeah, sure."

Kiddo: "That if you put them all together they would fill up nine football stadiums?"

Dad: "Gross."

Kiddo: "That no matter where you are, you're always within ten feet of a hundred spiders?"

Dad: "I did not know that."

Kiddo: "Neither did I. Until now."

And thus, a completely normal fascination morphed into a neurosis. I enrolled him into Boy Scouts to assuage his fear and teach him The Outdoors. This was a mistake. We arrived at Camp Stranglehold in the middle of summer when the heat and the rain had driven Michigan's insects into an orgiastic frenzy. The air was tumescent with nine bajillion varieties of OH MY GOD WHAT IS THAT?! Fear walked, crawled, wriggled, and leaped on six legs in a writhing, seething, buzzing, visible mass throughout the campsite. About three in the afternoon of the first day, the boy tries to ask for more pants, when something soft, pale, and prehistoric lands in his open mouth. He spit it out and it flew away like nothing had happened.

And here, friends, cohorts, fellow bad parents, is where you may recognize how my peculiar humor does not serve my progeny well. Instead of handing him my bottle of warm Kool-Aid, instead of patting him on the shoulder while offering a comforting chuckle, I said: "It's ok, it was just laying eggs."

And it did not get better. Late that night, after hours of carefully wrapping him in a cocoon of mosquito netting, after talking him down off the ledge into a doze, I laid my own head down on my cot and began to drift away. Just as I shifted into REM, the kid whispers across the tent, fully Blair Witched, "Dad, I have to pee."

Now please understand I am exhausted. I'm extricating myself from a deep sleep and I'm just not thinking. I open the mosquito netting, unmummify the boy in the dark, help him get his shoes on, click on the flashlight, slowly open the tent flaps, hand the light to the kid, and gently push him out.

Into screaming.

In the dancing circle of torchlight, the bugs crawling across the ground were so thick they looked like migrating wigs. Roon stopped screaming long enough to tell me he was peeing in the tent. I didn't stop him.

Today he was getting ready for school when I realized he'd been in the shower a long time.

Dad: "You ok?"

Son: [silence]

Dad: "Son!?"

Son: "I'm trapped."

Dad: "Whattaya mean?"

Son: "There's a spider. I saw it on the windowsill but now it's gone."

Dad: "Son, come out."

Son: "I DON'T KNOW WHERE IT IS!"

Dad: "It's ok, it's probably looking for water."

Son: [thrashing sounds]

DOMO ARAGATO

We're sending my son to Japan this summer.

We're not doing this because he deserves it—he doesn't. We're not doing this for his cultural edification (he's just going to buy "Engrish" T-shirts and play video games the entire time, we know that). We're not sending him because it's cheap cause, trust me, I could buy a modestly appointed vintage sports car with the swag we're blowing on this.

We're sending him because up until the moment his raggedy jeans plop down into the business class seat of that jet, we can, and will, dangle this priceless excursion in front of him like a forty-foot-tall, diamond-encrusted, solid gold carrot. We're doing it because he'll do anything to remain Japan worthy in our eyes.

And when I say anything, I mean he'll take out the trash after dark in the snow. Twice.

"Hey Roon, take down the Christmas lights."

"Aw, Dad, I'm in the middle of an Orc campaign!"

"Do you want to go to Japan?"

"You want them boxed by size or color?"

"Roon, go get those eight cases of Diet Coke out of the trunk."

"Dad, it's three in the morning and our lawn is crawling with rabid weasels!"

"Japan."

"Gimme the keys."

m

"Roon, climb up on the roof and wipe the snow off the satellite dish."

"But Dad—"

"*Konnichiwa.*"

"I'll get the ladder."

I don't even have to ask him anymore. I drop the subtlest of hints.

"Who invented Nintendo?"

"What's Godzilla's favorite food?"

"You know, we drive a Toyota."

And it works! This is a kid so lazy moss makes fun of him. He once took so long walking to school when he got there he was in the next grade. But now, I just serve him ramen noodles and he's on his feet dusting the credenza. He even comes to me with ideas, like an eager little subcontractor. It's awesome.

My house has never been so clean. My dishwasher has never been so loaded. My dog poop has never been so thoroughly picked up.

The truth is, I don't want him to go. I just want to stay here in my muumuu and teach him how to tend bar and do my expenses. I'm thinking about failing to make that final payment to the agency. Imagine what I might accomplish! I could get that new addition built. I could xeriscape the front yard.

I could get the laundry done.

But I can't. I . . . well . . . no; it's a bad idea. It's evil. I genuinely want him to have the time of his life, I do. Hell, I'm jealous.

But I can't help wondering what I'm going to hold over his head when he's back from Japan, sprawled in his gamer throne, jacked up on caffeine, and screaming into his headset? I might as well put a down payment on a trip to Ireland. Then, the moment he steps foot off that plane, I'll be all "top o' the mornin' to you, gov'nr" and feeding him brisket. He'll be all, "Dad that's awesome!" And I'll smile, tip my green felt top hat with my shillelagh, and tell him to get started on the roof.

VEGECONTRARIAN

As much as I applaud the anti-cruelty philosophy behind my son's vegetarianism, I'm beginning to suspect he doesn't entirely get that being a vegetarian means you have to eventually eat some vegetables.

I was thrilled when he told me he was a vegetarian. Ok, I was bemused when . . . Look: I was holding a pork shoulder I'd slow roasted all day. I put the pork down, looked him in the eye, and said, "You know this means you have to eat zucchini, right?"

It hasn't happened yet. So far my vegetarian's diet is ramen noodles, grilled cheese sandwiches, pizza, and *elote d' microwave*. I haven't seen a single green vegetable enter his mouth since he declared his unmeatfulness and I hold little hope that I will. It's not like I don't try. Witness our regular conversation. And by regular, I mean every seven minutes.

"Dad, I'm hungry."

"Awesome, how about some Brussels sprouts?"

"Dad, please be serious. I'm starving."

"Zucchini?"

"Yeah . . . no."

"Asparagus?"

"Dad."

"Spinach?"

"I had spinach last year."

He's a vegecontrarian! And he's definitely mature for his fourteen years. Most vegetarians don't get all political until they can drive because they need that first car for all the bumper stickers. Mine is constantly bringing up meat processing horror stories and asking me if I like the spleen bits in my hot dog (they're the best part, dammit).

Currently, we're in a standoff.

"Hey kid, I made instant udon noodles."

"Can't. They use fish products."

"Hot fries?"

"Fried in beef tallow."

"Wheat grass?"

"Buffalo walked through it."

"Gravel?"

"You scooped that out of the fish tank. I'm not stupid."

I've handed him tabouleh ("Ew!"), hummus ("Isn't that Latin for dirt?"), falafel ("Paper mâché meatballs."), and tofu ("Who sneezed in my stir fry?"). For a veggie, he's a tad particular.

Maybe I have little room to complain, as he's lost twelve pounds, his acne has cleared up, and he's spending a lot more time outside (probably foraging). Even our grill time is not entirely lost. I buy him "smeat" (soy based fake meat—as if Willy Wonka worked in produce), sign an affidavit that I scoured the grill of all meat remnants, then grill it right alongside my rib-eyes.

And I taunt, I taunt mercilessly because I hate that he's a vegetarian. I don't care if you think it's unsupportive, we're talking U.S.D.A. here, people, we're talking bacon. We took some visiting relatives to Gene & Georgetti's. I ordered a lightly seared full-grown steer. As I looked across the expanse of burnt flesh before me, I watched my son pick at a wan pasta-based afterthought and look wistfully askance.

Is it mean? Look, I don't know. Maybe. But there're two ways this can go: I can taunt him into giving up his hippy stance, wherein he will actually eat broccoli as an accompaniment to a New York strip, or he will get fed up and start shoveling green things into his mouth just to show me he means business. Everybody wins.

SPERM WAIL

Today I walked out onto the Mother Theresa tarmac to retrieve Boy and saw him from all the way across the lot, beaming at me, loaded with promise. What a moment. I mean, he's like a little Kennedy doll and he's picked me out, made eye contact, from like fifty yards, and I know he's just bursting with pride. It's like he's barely containing a nuclear bomb of pride and I'm so glad. I could use it.

I had a bad day. My Mac deep-sixed at THE VERY MOMENT I WAS UPLOADING A CLIENT'S FINISHED WEBSITE. I mean like as my finger hovered over the return key, as the space between the fingerprints and the Belleek china surface of the Mac grew increasingly smaller, until I could practically feel the nano-indentation of the word "Enter," the screen froze and my Mac died it's third and least noble death.

I absorbed the brunt of the snot gargling this week and received my dubious infection like a church wafer, spending most of yesterday lying in bed watching *Top Chef* re-reruns and wondering if I had the temerity to stand erect in the shower long enough to shave (I didn't). I actually went to the store in my "cold clothes"—cut-off-jersey-raggy-old-shorts that look like I cleaned a crime scene in them with a matching T-shirt complete with espresso-tinged ellipses running down my front like some weird T-shirt semaphore, a semiotic self-referential version of

"I'm with stupid," the kind of high-end, hyper-intelligent garb Umberto Eco would wear to a microbrew ten-pin bowling alley old-school martini joint.

And my guitar was out of tune.

And my headlight went out.

And did I mention my Mac had crashed? I mean, I had just spent something like eight hours crunching through a Flash site from scratch, turning it into a beeeautiful work of art that screamed through transitions and just looked gorgeous—for free. And can't. Show. It to any. Body.

And I got bad customer service from the Mac store. This is what kills me. The Mac store, my place of worship, middle managemented me. I know the face, I've worked retail. I know when I've hit the customer service terminal wall.

So walking across the hot sticky tar (90° in September!) and seeing my son broadcasting a radiant ear-to-ear and knowing that he's at this top-shelf school and knowing that he's finally working at the level he deserves, I'm thinking he's going to say something like:

Father, Dear, you were right! *The Brothers Karamazov* really is incredible!

Or:

Wow—the similarities between Latin and English are stunning. Did you know . . .

Or, even:

I owned pre-calc today!

Because your kid, smiling, smart, achieving, can blow the bad day away. That genuine enthusiasm, the kind of all-in, yeah-baby, crash-the-car bravado that only kids can provide, can clear it all out like a fire hose. Reset. Do over.

And that's what I wanted. And just like any good *Wuthering Heights* remake, I loped in slowmo across the blacktop to my prideful, beside-himself with accomplishment, scion of fifth grade intelligentsia, fruit of my loins, heir to my . . . fortune. Mini me, my boy, drops in beside me and says:

"Dude, today we totally talked about sperm!"

HOME ALONE, DUDE

My wife and I had to go out of town.

While engaging in the NASA-level logistics required by travel, our recently teened son volunteered to stay behind to watch the house and menagerie, causing my wife and I to swoon after realizing the money we'd save on pet sitters, house sitters, and someone to maintain surveillance on our Canadian neighbors.

I would like to report that at this juncture, as professional parents, we sat down for a long talk with the kid about responsibilities and curfews, but all I remember is arriving breathless and poorly packed at O'Hare. We were somewhere over Ohio when we looked at each other and realized what we'd done.

"I bet he's on fire right now."

"The dogs are gonna starve."

"It's OK, they'll probably eat his corpse."

We worried through a hideous parade of catastrophes until the plane landed. I called him immediately.

"ARE YOU OK?"

"Dad, I'm in the middle of a game. When are you guys leaving?"

This held us over through renting a car, but as soon as we

were on the road, hellish visions of disaster struck again. What if the pilot light goes out? What if a plane crashes on our house? What if he gets a tattoo? We pulled over.

"CHECK THE STOVE!"

"Dad, seriously. I'm in an Orc campaign. People depend on me. You guys have to learn how to be on your own."

He was right. We had spent fourteen years turning him into the remarkably responsible young man he had become. He knew how to run the house, take care of pets, order Chinese. Really, truthfully, except for bartending and finances, our work was done. He was fine.

So we did what any confident, highly accomplished parents do. We forgot about him.

Two days of micro-seminars and macro-martinis later, I get a call.

"Dad, did you leave your office light on?"

"No, I—"

"I think there's a burglar."

"If there was a burglar, the dogs would be—wow, the dogs are really barking, aren't they?"

"I'm 99.9 percent sure it's OK, but I'm going upstairs to check."

"What if there is a burglar?"

"It's OK, I have a knife."

Abrupt signal loss.

As a parent, 800 miles away in the middle of nowhere with a bad connection and overactive imagination, I can tell you I was jumpy. My kid's shoe size is listed as Sasquatch. He ducks under doors. He can pick up a car. However, he is unduly skittish. His reaction to spiders, for instance, is insanely comical—like he's doing yoga really fast. Plus he's clumsy.

So my vision of him confronting a burglar with a knife ended with multiple self-inflicted stab wounds and a note from the crook: "Dear parents, What is wrong with you people?"

I shot out of the conference into the rain, fear tears streaming down my face, sealing contracts with various lesser deities, apologizing to the great wheel of karma for leaving my only son home alone, pointing my phone into the stratosphere for bars, when he called back, his voice tight with urgency.

"DAD! DAD! OH MY GOD! DAD!"

"OH SWEET JESUS, BOY, WHAT IS IT!?"

"There's no more frozen pizza!"

They say a sound was heard that night, in the far reaches of the North Carolina hills near a conference center, a snarling, depraved, nearly human wail, guttural, almost forming words. They say it might be proof that Sasquatch lives.

I can assure you: *Not for long*.

MY SON'S ABIDING LOVE FOR JUSTIN BIEBER

My son misses school a lot. Or, he did, until I discovered the awesome power of sick notes.

Now he won't stay home even if he's bleeding and on fire. He'd rather expire in the nurse's office than have to turn in one of these:

To whom it may concern: Please excuse Roon for his absence Nov. 1, as he was working on his *port de bras*. Allow him extra time between classes as he will be practicing his *battement fondu*. Also, do you sell tutus in school colors? Go Tigers! *Entrechat!*

To whom it may concern: Please excuse Roon's absence Oct. 9. He was severely ill after eating a significant volume of library paste.

To whom it may concern: Roon was absent Sept. 14 after receiving multiple needle gun wounds in Halo 3. He re-spawned later in the day. Alas, too late to make it to school on time.

To whom yadda yadda yadda: Roon was late today because he was trapped in the shower by a spider. I urge caution when approaching him, he's kind of jumpy.

People, listen: Roon was late Tuesday because we couldn't find a McDonald's that had cinnamon buns. We went to four different drive-thrus. Also, we ran out of gas.

To whom: Spiders again.

Please excuse Roon for his absence Monday as he was recovering. Early Monday morning, he went into his closet and was attacked by dirty jeans and underwear. He held them off as long as he could with a music stand, but they finally outnumbered him and he went down.

Roon could not attend school Thursday because of his deep and abiding love for the music of Justin Bieber.

Roon was late Monday after getting stuck in the Downward Facing Dog pose during his morning disco yoga routine. I tried to use a leash to bring him, but he bit my hand. His vet says to keep him away from other kids for a week.

Roon was not absent last week. He had his name legally changed to Help Me Rhonda, Help Help Me Rhonda but the forms never made it to your school. Please change his name in your records and refer to him by this name at all times.

THE GUESS WHAT CHICKEN BUTT CONTINUUM

If he says it one more time, I will kill him. This is not hyperbole. I have cause, just cause, to take him out—my son, the new teenager, the purveyor of the non sequitur, the little !@#$#% who thinks this is the pinnacle of high comedy:

"Dad, guess what?"

Wait, let me stop right here. You need context for this to make sense. You have to know the buoyant hope with which I unconsciously respond to my son; you need to envision his beatific dome turning to me in the car, a smile on his face that can melt steel, a sparkle in his eye foretelling outstanding accomplishment, recognition, genuine inspiration.

"Dad, guess what?"

I mean, you have to believe, the way I always believe, that this time, this grin, this smirk, is heartfelt. This time it's not a sucker's bet. You have to let your mind unspool histrionic scenarios of potential greatness: He's on the honor roll; he got picked as valedictorian; he invented Flubber.

"Dad, guess what?"

You have to be standing there elbow deep in sink-water splendor thinking about your other life, the one wherein you stand with an insouciant slouch against the dark mahogany bar of a private club that is feting your recent literary—

"Dad, guess what?"

You have to be hauling a bag of dog food up onto your shoulder, envisioning yourself trim and well-jeaned, worn flannel sleeves rolled up, neighborhood soccer moms slowing down their minivans and thinking how lucky Mrs.—

"Dad, guess what?"

You have to be on your knees in the laundry room fishing underwear out of the dryer vent and wondering how in the name of God—I mean, how is it even possible? Did the underwear pull the lint screen out? Did they transmogrify themselves into the—

"Dad, guess what?"

You have to be asleep, deep into the dream about the mahogany bar, Don Draper just finishing his riveting extemporaneous speech lauding your singular character, rolling it into a metaphor about scotch, people crying, the reporter from *Life* magazine applauding, and you—

"Dad, guess what?"

You have to be hunkered over your old Royal, like an anvil with buttons, your mind reeling with the pure, unadulterated beauty, the sheer mind-bending brilliance of the first sentence of your first screenplay, when the main character—a perfect blend of Cary Grant, Tom Hanks, and Bruce Campbell—looks into the camera and says—

"Dad, guess what?"

WHAT!? WHAT?! FOR THE LOVE OF ALL THINGS HOLY— WHAT? WHAT? WHAT? WHAT? WHAAAAAAAT?!!!!

"Chicken butt!"

PICTURE DAY

I was going through pictures of my son the other day. For most people, this is a heartwarming experience. There's a cup of coffee, a scrapbook, and the morning light filtered through the living room windows. For me, it means scrolling on my cell phone through a near infinite collection of perfect portraits of his right hand.

He hates getting his picture taken. I have exactly seven blurry snapshots of his face: one is half obscured by his Sasquatchian paw, and the rest are tiny portraits dominated by the inside of his mouth, the cover of a book, his shirt pulled over his nose, and a single unadulterated head shot in which it is painfully obvious he's farting.

My only hope has been Picture Day. And as I am a diligently organized parent with a smart phone, a computer, a notebook, a Day-Timer, and a watch, I never know it's Picture Day until Sasquatch is getting out of the car whereupon he will lean in, as if to say something sweet.

Imagine: Framed in the window with the sun behind him like a halo, his "Legalize It" T-shirt hanging in a stained, pouchy slouch, a tiny smear of grape jelly trailing off toward his ear, and his unruly Aboriginal dome, and he says: "Oh yeah, it's Picture Day."

Merde! Fantastic. I will add this new abomination to the

growing aggregation of legendary school portraits wherein Junior appears...

- to have been dragged backwards through a bush

- under anesthesia

- over-caffeinated

- infused with pure, unalloyed evil

I could scrapbook a three-inch brick of Disney pictures of our family smiling with the radiant intensity of an Osmond wedding, and in each of them will be a perfect picture of Roon's hand where his head should be. My only clear picture of his face shows him slumped face first into the couch, his nose bent sideways in a puddle of drool (I assume), with the dog frenching his ear.

I can only hope, as he enters high school, he will start combing his hair and washing his face the morning of Picture Day after discovering girls might want a picture of his actual face. I mean, he's a good-looking kid. I think. I don't know, all I see is hair.

Until that time, like every other parent of a teen boy, I lurk in the living room until I hear snoring, tip toe into his room, peel back his hideous mop, gaze into his face and think to myself: *Yes, that's him, thank God.*

THAT'S MY BOY?

There were times I wasn't sure my son belonged to me. I worried perhaps there'd been a mix up in maternity, like maybe one of the nurses held my actual son in her arms, his cherubic mug illuminating the entire ward, then looked at me and thought, "This can't be right. Give him the trucker baby!"

My infant son was unlike me in so many ways my friends insisted we'd adopted.

First, he was gorgeous. Seriously, he was a good-looking baby. He'd make women swoon in the produce aisle; strangers were compelled to pick him up and then, as I wrestled him out of their hands, they'd look at me—an unholy mash-up of Jack Black and Philip Seymour Hoffman's uglier brother—and refuse to give him back.

Like they were saving him.

Secondly, his head is huge. I can't take the kid downtown; people start following us because THEY THINK WE'RE A PARADE!

The disparity really becomes clear when I can't take it anymore and I turn to drink. Then my son shows his true nature: street preacher. Where my inner child is a drug-crazed, beer-addicted Hobbit, his is an angry, implacable Amish preacher who will catch me sneaking a PBR in the pantry, raise his bony little fist, and decry, "BEER IS DRUGS, DAD!"

I'm not entirely convinced he's mine. I mean, I'm suspicious, but it's tempered by the still moments, the graceful, accidental snapshots when he rolls his head into my shoulder and falls asleep or when he's whispering poop jokes in my ear and then laughs so hard he pees his pants—these are the hard arguments for him being mine.

And, yeah, he's cute and he's no fan of beer (yet), but most of his life is made of these candid instants, these stunning, high-resolution memories of nothing special, when he's not paying attention and I know, like some kind of radiant signal pinging through my brain, without question this is me duplicated.

The other day I heard him on the back porch, his melodic voice angelic in its clarity, like a little bell, singing in Latin. In Latin. I hid in the kitchen trying to stifle a little tear of pride, trying to take it in, to internalize just how brilliant this kid is, silently high-fiving nobody, until I couldn't stand it and asked him what Latin prayer he was singing.

"You're stupid, Dad. It's *Dora the Explorer*."

So, yeah. He's mine.

MY SON'S AWESOME BALLS

Sports are not my thing. They never have been. Unless someone invents the 100-yard smartass, I'm never going to win any athletic competition. I never played football, never played basketball, never freaked out over a fantasy football draft, never wrestled. I was on a forensics team for like one day—and I played Little League.

Now my son is playing baseball and he's into it like he's falling off a cliff. We've spent a grand total of fourteen million dollars outfitting him with digital socks, a laser guided mitt, Kevlar penis armor, and training equipment including personal visits from White Sox players and the ghost of Babe Ruth. As I directed the wagon train of teamsters to the register at Sports Authority, I realized youth baseball is a racket and I'm its biggest sucker.

But I don't care. I'll spend another million tomorrow because my son is into it. He's all about the baseball. He eats sunflower seeds, spits, hustles his huevos on the baseline, fidgets with his hat, keeps his foot on the bag, dusts his hands, and checks the air flow . . . and disco dances.

I remember Little League. I remember left field. I remember no kids could ever put it out there and if they did the third baseman (showoff) would be under it before I could even start running, so I mostly stared at the traffic and ate mulberries from an absolutely gargantuan mulberry tree. The mulberries on this thing were as long as my middle finger and I'd come in from defense with purple stains on my Owls uniform. So I know all about the boredom of left field. I assume it's the same in right. It must be because in his game yesterday, Roon wasn't staring through the gap between second and first at the batter and chattering like a steely-eyed White Sox player. He was busting a move.

When I say he was busting a move, I mean he was John Travolting. You could tell by the way he used his walk. It didn't last long, and as I was sitting next to one of the most charmingly unabashed Scout moms in the world, whom I've known long enough that she wouldn't hesitate to punch me on the shoulder and scream, *hey, look at your gay son*, I know no one else saw it. But *I* did. It's burned into my mind: a spastic hip-pumping, finger-pointing, head-shaking, *Staying Alive* poster emulating jig right there in right field, and I know it was totally spontaneous and I know he's going to do it again. *I know it*.

The Roon likes the disco. He routinely erupts into a hip-thrusting, ten-year-old boy version of *Bad* by Michael "I Live In Bahrain Cause They Won't Arrest Me Here"[2] Jackson that, in my day, would get his ass kicked faster than wearing a tutu. Worse, it makes him laugh, and when Roon laughs, his bones turn into Jell-O and he falls down.

So here's what I'm looking at: it'll be the big game in the clutch and Roon'll be playing first base. The other coach will have a brief talk with his next batter up giving Roon just enough time for his mind to wander and he'll forget where he is and he'll spaz

[2] Written before Mr. Jackson moonwalked off this mortal coil.

out into his John Travolta Tourette's Syndrome thing, realize he's doing it, start laughing, and fall down just as the third baseman throws the ball to clinch a triple play and it sails over his prone, wiggling, possibly urinating form.

At least he's happy.

MY SON'S AWESOME BALLS 2

Another Man Moment slides into oblivion as I ponder my son's recently acquired balls.

We were at the Sox–Yankees game at Comiskey Park, just south of Chinatown, here in Chicago, sitting in seats good enough for God. My son had brought his glove, a ball, and a Sharpie. We were twenty rows up from the Sox dugout, looking down the first baseline from home plate. Roon and I grabbed the Sharpie and the gear and loped down the steps to the dugout where Jenks signed our stuff. It was sunny and nippy and the guy selling hot dogs was saying it like it was some kind of verdant truth. He didn't call out, "HOOOOOT DOOOOOGSS!" like they usually do. He glared into the crowd, banged on his box, and stated, perfunctorily: "Hot Dogsh." Like he was saying, "They ain't hot pretzels, Idiot."

So Roon is sitting there burning in the sun, and he has his little black glove and his Sox hat and his Sox shirt, and Mockoviak slices one to eight o'clock and guess who gets it? Oh, yeah. The guy RIGHT BEHIND MY SON. Roon had his hand in the air and it tipped his glove and shot into the open hands of the baseball marketing director sitting behind us.

This has happened before. We were at a Bulls game and one of those impossibly curvaceous T-shirt girls slingshots a Bulls shirt into the air over our heads. Its parachute opened and it drifted down like some kind of modified Chinese water torture specialty, like a Fellini take, like for seven and a half years it floated down directly over my son's head. There's no one around us for like fourteen seats and he's screaming. I mean BELLOWING, "I GOT IT, I GOT IT" and just as it's almost in his hands the wind (wind?) blows it one seat back to a guy in a suit (AT A FRIKKING BALL GAME). I just turned around and stared down into his brainstem for a second and he smiled and handed the shirt to Roon who proceeded to scream until his throat blew out.

But it was different at the Sox game. The guy had class. He didn't even hesitate. He shoved it into Roon's glove, said "Nice catch, kid! GO SOX!" and patted him on the back. Roon was practically weightless. He held the thing up and whooped with the kind of unadulterated glee that made my inner Southern boy proud.

After the game (Sox pasted the Yankees), we walked out and Roon carried the ball in front of him and kept saying to me, "It sure is cool that I caught this foul ball, huh? Yep, caught a foul ball, right here. Yep, this one. Nice one dad, huh? This foul ball? This ball? That I caught?" All the way down six levels until we were in the car. Then he rolled the window down. "I sure like this ball. This ball is super cool, this foul ball. That I caught."

Ahh. Baseball.

THE GIRL

Being a man, I am, and always will be, unqualified to raise a girl. First of all, my daughter's smarter than me. She can see right through me. For a little while Rah thought I was king of the world and knew everything. But as life went on she would glance over at her mom, who would shake her head and roll her eyes, and eventually the girl caught on. Now I'm just furniture.

I am from the generation whose moms burned their bras and

got jobs as crane operators and CEOs. They began the leveling process that will (one day) see women paid the same as men, women recognized as professionals in exactly the same way as men, and men giving birth. So it is no surprise that my daughter simply does not see her future as a housewife, or a seamstress (whatever that is), or even a bank teller. She sees herself becoming a rock star astronaut spy. Or she did. Now I think she's trying to become a brain surgeon/graphic artist/costume designer, but I'm not sure. She's locked in her room and there's music playing. Loudly.

The great thing about being a man and raising a post-suffragette daughter is seeing her live the rock star life she deserves. She's a pink and blue haired, curse capable, frankly belching organ of purpose and success. Should any assbackward grizzled old jerk ever stand between her and a promotion and dare to say something about kitchens, inappropriate footwear, and pregnancy, she'll break off his arms and beat him to death with them. I'm pretty damn proud of that.

THE THINGS WE DO FOR LOVE

I'd like to set the record straight: I am a large, hairy, tattooed man with a dad-face that can level small import cars at thirty yards. I have scowled my way through some hairy situations with just a dirty T-shirt and the pure annealed anger I carry in the core of my soul like every other American male. I'm not telling you that to brag about my manliness, I'm telling you this so you understand I don't normally get pedicures.

I don't normally get pedicures.

But a father is a warrior. A father is a fighter. A father is a ninja. Because our kids are half-pint psychofreaks that can snap any second. Particularly the teens. Particularly the girls. My girl was feeling particularly flippity-floppity recently and, in the slump of a blue funk, talked her mom into therapeutic shopping.

We were tooling through the mall when the girls swerved mid-retail and lit out for the nail salon territories. And here's where I went wrong. I should have let them go. I was standing in front of a bar. I should have blown them a kiss and ordered scotch. Like a man. Instead, I said this: "You're just leaving me here?" And thus, the pivotal comedy relief montage in a father–daughter afternoon special was born—starring *moi*.

My pedicurist, Dorothy, attacked my feet as if they'd made her mad. With instruments. Then she tickled me. Then she went into the kitchen and got a cheese grater and a blowtorch, and after a half hour and a lot of cursing (I assume...it was all in Korean and it did not sound poetic), she gave up and quit her job.

And here's where I made my next mistake. The angry woman kneeling at my feet asked me what color I wanted. Look, despite the foot attack, getting a pedicure is remarkably relaxing and I was sort of drifting at this point and just hooked a thumb over at my girl and said, "Whatever she gets."

In retrospect, this was not well considered. My daughter chose to paint my toenails THEY CAN NEVER SEE THIS AT FISHCAMP PINK. With sparkly hearts.

It gets worse: Who knew under the grime and the horny plates and wire I had pretty feet? I haven't seen them since 1998 and I was very, very surprised to see they'd made the difficult decision to change gender. Still, I embraced their supple pink glint and flip-flopped my way over to the manicure table where Dorothy gave me a lecture about hangnails and stabbed me in my palm.

Afterwards, we dropped the girl off at school and went back to our lives. At first, I was sheepish. I was slightly embarrassed. I didn't know what to do with my new cute feet. When the plumber came to fix the sink, I made him wait on the porch in the cold while I frantically searched for something to cover my bejeweled metatarsals. I met him wearing dirty gym shorts and a pair of $150 dress shoes. Now, I don't care. The Orkin guy was here this morning and I met him at the door fully Lebowskied. My toes beaming out from under my tattered robe, rosy beacons for ridicule, a precious version of "Do you feel lucky, Punk?" Because trust me, they are provocative. And to my various neighbors: If I shuffle out to get my paper just as you pass by with your man-purse dog and your triple macchiato and you try to iPhone my gorgeous peds, you better be packing. There is nothing more macho, nothing more rugged, nothing more Eastwood, than displaying one's decorous digits to the world after getting them done because your daughter needed it and the look on her face afterwards could melt diamonds. So go ahead. *Say something.*

These are not just painted toes. They are badges of extreme fathering. Not everything about being a great parent is dramatic and not everything is paint by numbers. Sometimes, the things we do for love are pink and filled with glittery hearts.

MY EYES BURNED OUT BY BOOBS— MERRY CHRISTMAS!

My daughter turns fourteen in less than a month. She is distressingly beautiful and walks with a confidence and dominion I can barely get together even now, at forty-two years old. I can't imagine what it must be like to be thirteen years old and have this kind of aplomb. I adore her and I will brag ad infinitum (ask anybody). But I'm having a hard time accepting that fourteen is on the downhill side of little girl. This was made alarmingly clear this holiday season when my daughter asked for and received a really expensive dress. When I say really expensive dress, just think of it more like a fancy word for traveling boob display case.

I'm not really an old-fashioned dad. I can't be. I'm the mom. I do the dishes, manage the homework, cook the meals, clean the house, and drive. I quit my job in retail a while back so my wife could join the dark side as a patent attorney. I see her for all of eleven minutes a week. I am the quintessential soccer mom, except that I'm a man and we do basketball.

Being a man means having habits and appreciations and thoughts that are significantly different from homemakers of olde. I, for instance, don't know squat about girls. Never have. Dating was a total disaster for me until I met my wife, and she sat down with me and explained, once, why I was such an unmitigated butthead with women, and that if I ever wanted to see her naked, I should do a, b, and c, and never d or e again, and don't even think about the rest of the alphabet. God bless her. So my daughter has been a walking mystery my whole life, and since she hit puberty (like a truck full of dynamite slamming into a BP) and received her mystical woman-sight, she realized I was just another stupid jerk boy and she pretty much quit worshipping me. I'm just a big, fat, hairy jerkwad now, only good for getting stuff off the higher shelves and charging her iPod. Opening my mouth elicits eye rolling so violent and powerful I fully expect her to need a neck brace.

But my lack of gurrl knowledge is a convenient blind spot for a lot of things, most of all the fact that girls tend to turn into women, which means that at some point they sprout boobs. Of course I knew this would happen. In fact, it's been happening since she pubernated, but I rarely think about them, uh, it. In fact, my mind takes such elaborate routes to avoid the very concept of Daughter Boobs that it's like she's blurry between her waist and neck. I see nostrils and kneecaps—that's it.

On Christmas Day my daughter got her dress and promptly put it on. She'd just gotten her first haircut in God knows how long, a haircut administered on the sly by a woman who runs a booth on Michigan Avenue for a well-known department store so hoity-toity its name can't properly be pronounced without an ounce of black caviar in your mouth. Her hair was Jennifer Aniston good.

The dress I can only describe as a brown crinoline strapless poufy thing that must've required nanotechnology to get it on and looked like it was designed to invoke all the best parts of the

1944 Academy Awards banquet while simultaneously providing a level and architecturally sound platform for displaying my daughter's winnebagoes.

When I stumbled down the stairs and threw open the door, and my daughter turned to say good morning while wearing her new dress and whirling her Jennifer hair, I automatically submitted to the architecture of the dress and planted my eyes exactly where its engineers intended while simultaneously realizing, "Those belong to my daughter," whereupon my eyeballs exploded and a little voice in my head that sounded suspiciously like Charleston Heston whispered: *You, Sir, disgust me.*

I said, "Jesus, Rah, put those away!" And here's where things really got weird. My daughter was not only not embarrassed, she realized instantly that she wielded some kind of awesome power over me and, instead of demurely tugging up the edge of her expensive haute couture, she loomed her boobs in my direction and said, "Look, Dad, booooooobs," then cackled gleefully as I covered my eyes. She *cackled!*

Although, by degrees, my sight is returning, I have to say: my eyes were opened. I finally get that my daughter, though only fourteen, is pretty much grown. More importantly, I have had to take an objective, neutral look at her and accept that she's not only grown, she's drop dead beautiful, smarter than most of the adults I know, highly confident, and working on a kind of wisdom you don't expect from an eighth grader. She's the kind of girl that makes boys run into things and, while they are addled and trying get upright, she has the capacity, and, I bet, the will, to talk them into doing anything she wants, from moving furniture to investing in bio-tech. Should she decide to follow in her mother's footsteps and go into law, I have no doubt she will be like some kind of Greek-god force of nature and make ten bajillion dollars before she's thirty.

And I suddenly realize what this means. It isn't just that she's sporting new equipment. It's bigger than that. She's coming into her own, assuming the mantle of her glamour in a time when there are no restrictions on her gender. The fight has pretty much been won. And instead of the fugly, hairy-legged, braless skanks men feared would come out of the ERA, we've got my daughter: super gorgeous, highly educated, and bristling with glamorous regard. I fear for the poor bastards who get in her way.

DRIVING MISS CRAZY

I have stared into the gaping, drooly maw of death. I have teetered on the brink of imminent demise. Now, every day is a gift. I take time to smell the cappuccino. I live in the moment not worrying about tomorrow because yesterday, I tried to teach my ADD daughter how to drive.

I prepared myself for this ordeal like any pragmatic father of a girl who can't pay attention to an entire commercial: I dialed 911 on my cell; I hugged my wife and told her where to send a search team; I made an ice-cold dirty martini.

I didn't want her to drive. This is a girl who can get distracted while tying her shoes. Letting her pilot a 5,000-pound hurtling tank of flammable gas through our neighborhood strikes me as unpragmatic. It makes me wish we were Amish.

For the sake of other parents in this predicament, some cautions:

1. *Closed course:* We used a forest preserve lot. No one goes there except forest preserve cops and the escaped convicts they're looking for.

   Pro: No oncoming cars.

   Con: Deer, and they're pretty! So brace yourself for sudden screeching halts followed closely by a barrage of "oh-my-god-that-deer-is-soooooo-gorgeous" moments.

2. *Midnight run:* Like this kid sleeps. Might as well take advantage of the deserted, well-lit streets and clock some time while everyone else is watching The Late Show.

   Con: The adrenalin making your heart spaz-out like a highly caffeinated chihuahua as your daughter drifts into the other lane to see if the couple in the next car are breaking up will keep you awake until three a.m.

   Pro: If you get a flat, you can lift the car with one hand.

3. *Catch phrases:* Once she sees that one kid with the long hair and the pierced nose slouching on a bus bench as you hurl past, a lengthy explanation about lane obedience will most likely be punctuated by death. Better to have a short punchy catchphrase at the ready. Mine was "color in the lines," which works best when delivered in all caps, thusly: "COLOR IN THE LINES! COLOR IN THE LINES! OH MY GOD, WE'RE GOING TO DIE!"

   Pro: Short and easy to scream.

   Con: Whiplash.

4. *Frank Sinatra:* The sheer bravado and *élan* in a good Sinatra song soothes nerves and bolsters confidence. Might work on the kid, too.

   Pro: Goes well with the martini.

   Con: Goes well with the martini.

These are just a few ideas, of course. I'd give more but my nerves are shot, and I'm still in the middle of calling close relatives and letting them know I'm alive.

THE SECRET LIFE OF FATHERS AND DAUGHTERS FINALLY REVEALED IN ALL ITS EVIL SPLENDOR

[My Attorney] works at home sometimes. Her MO is to sit down on our slouch, pull the piano bench in front of her, open up the latest *American Idol*, and start working. That's about the time her Blackberry vibrates off the bench and scurries across the carpet, its contents a volatile email with attached documents demanding that she solve the legal equivalent of Fermat's Last Theorem within the hour. Suddenly Randy is frozen mid-*dawg* and [My Attorney]'s hands go up like shields and the household is admonished to, "SHUSSSH!"

Now, because we respect the sheer magnitude and complexity of what it is (*whatever* it is) [My Attorney] does, the kids and I generally respect her wishes, drop everything, and start disco dancing. We'll keep it up, pumping and thrusting like our life depends on it, until she screams and grabs her head and cries out in anguish, "YOU PEOPLE ARE SO WEIRD!"

This morning, her Blackberry throbbed like a quarter-fed hotel bed, shot off the table, and stabbed [My Attorney] in the forehead, whereupon she ripped a leg off the table and threatened the 14-year-old-95th-percentile-ISAT-tester-Anime-superfan and me with bodily injury if we so much as breathed deep while she gnawed her arm off to get out of some bear-trap-legal-document deadline crisis. Rah and I were eating Captain Crunch before she went to school. Our eyes were unfixed and wobbling in our heads—her's because she's a teen and mine because I broke my coffeemaker—when [My Attorney]'s urgent outburst snapped us to attention. We looked at each other and, reading each other's minds, started tapping our spoons against the edges of our bowls.

It started out as just a mildly snarky jab, but as we gazed into each other's eyes, our inherent malice leaked out like burning tar, and our light tapping morphed from synchronized cereal consumption normalcy, directly through "let's raise our glass for a toast" wine glass clanging, all the way to a Niebelung anvil hammering cacophony of seismic proportions.

Gleefully evil.

Maybe I shouldn't be proud of how my girl-spawn so easily slides into maliciousness, but I am deeply pleased that we have that silent Vulcan mind-meld, and I am even more deeply pleased—my joy, in fact, is boundless—at the knowledge that this psychic connection is rooted in mutual sarcasm.

TRUE LOVE ATE MY HOMEWORK

Well it happened. The girl-child finally got a boyfriend. This is big news and a mountain-sized moment as she's been coveting the status of "boyfriended" since birth.

I knew that a high school filled with drama queens and ultra geeks would be the place for her to find her soul mate, and that's why I sent her there. Other kids see this high school, which might as well be called "Super Hero High," as an academic Mecca, a math-and-science Matterhorn, and face each day with the necessary resolve to fight their way through the high-concept classes to the goal of good grades.

But not the girl. When we were leaving orientation, starry-eyed and blown away by the sheer Hogwartsian quality of the place, my daughter was floating on air for an entirely different reason. We saw a level of academia you rarely see in good colleges, much less in a high school. But Rah crunched her packet to her chest and sighed, "Did you see all the cute boys in there? Oh my GOD!"

There were a couple of false starts, a Ziggy–Marleyan young man who was far too forgiving of my daughter's various insanities, telescoping his base hopes a little too clearly; and some French kid who apparently didn't like her misuse of post-participle noun-events but thought she had pretty eyes. She waved them both off, saw right through them, left them floundering in the wasteland of IM "ignore" commands and a flurry of *whatevers*. But the third kid had a quality they didn't have in that he's very honest and very natural and when she was acting like a hyperactive, stage-hungry little nutcase he called her on it. And I think that mattered to her.

Then he kissed her.

So they're a couple. And by couple, I mean they disgust me. Last night the girl child gasped and flopped herself down on the end of the couch with such ridiculous force I thought she'd popped a rib. I paused the TV and asked her what happened. She sighed and said, "[undisclosed] sat here." I suppressed the sudden urge to vomit and was about to tell her she was being hyper dramatic but the Artist, who was leaning against the wall sipping tea, snorted and said, "Yeah, maybe some of his butt particles are still there," which you would think would snap the girl-child out of her love induced reverie but, no, she merely sighed again and said, "butt particles," and the rest of us rolled our eyes so hard the earth shifted in its orbit.

I had to drop her off at Hogwarts yesterday since [My Attorney] was in D.C. taking a dep (I love talking law, I feel like I'm on some cool TV show). On the way we listened to the new Eagles song, and dug it, and then Weezer's *Beverly Hills* came on, so we were rocking it in traffic, and she remembered she'd forgotten some homework and begged me to let her miss first period. I pulled over and let her out, told her to tell them her homework was a casualty of love.

I've dreaded this day as long as she's been aching for it, but I have to say it was anti-climactic. It didn't even bother me when I caught them entangled on the couch. I just told them to disentangle themselves and that was that. When she floated home the first day in love, I hugged her and said, "good for you." I didn't admonish her for snogging in the hallways. I didn't tell her to watch his hands. It never occurred to me. I was just happy for her.

Of course I put a tracking device in the kid's backpack while he wasn't looking, but that's just typical dad stuff. Right?

HOW TO FOLD YOUR DAUGHTER'S THONG

Being a stay-at-home dad has its advantages. I watch TV while I work. I listen to the stereo real loud. There's beer. The downside is the long suffered horror all moms know: There are no secrets.

You go through everyone's drawers. You wash their clothes. You sweep under their bed.

You fold your daughter's thong.

Look, I'm a ninja-level pop. I will go into Walgreens and inquire as to the location of the heavy-flow pads. Long ago I suffered through the horror of my daughter's emergent boobs.

But a thong in the laundry is a new horror.

My first impression was, "Oooh la la, Mommy for the win!" Mere seconds later I realized my voluptuous wife couldn't get this miniscule strap around her foot, much less up to her—OH MY GOD! My second impression was, OH MY GOD!

Unlike a bra, which, no matter how much black lace or pink ribbons it has, still is structurally important, a thong has no practical use except to say to the world, "I am legally not naked," which only happens in situations where someone else is—OH MY GOD!

We dads can work our minds around most daughter stuff. We plan ahead for puberty (beer), driving lessons (beer), and boyfriends (gun).

But we forget. Our little princesses are exploding out of puberty into unparalleled womanhood. Never in the history of man have women been so unfettered and free. They are the fortunate great-grandchildren of women's rights. They grew up in a world of equality, highly paid women CEOs, Oprah, and porn for girls.

Thank God for my golf skills. Using a seven iron, I carried my daughter's thong upstairs, like a dead rat on a skewer.

I was halfway across the living room when she walked in.

At this juncture, the highly educated father would employ a sports maneuver that snatched the panties out of sight before either of us needed to acknowledge them.

Most.

"You dropped your floss."

"Father, why are you hoisting my unmentionables into the air like a flag?"

"I'm surrendering."

ABSOLUTELY SUPER SARAH

When my little girl was a little girl, she wanted the same, simple, uncluttered, and achievable future every little girl desires: to be a ninja rock star princess spy. While most of that fell along the wayside as she blew through her days, she did accomplish one of her goals. Briefly, for a day, for an afternoon, my daughter was the greatest superhero the world has ever known.

Being a young lady of the post-information-age age, my daughter, Sarah, knew she had to have some accessories if she was to be a proper super hero. First on the list was a cape. Next was a logo. Third was a catchy name.

Being an old man of the pre-information-post-information-transition age, I knew this was kind of awesome. (At three and a half, she already knew the importance of marketing.) But first: a cape.

A pillowcase was quickly dispatched. I tied it around her neck and she launched herself into the stratosphere, flying around the living room and kitchen in a low orbit, making shushing noises as she skimmed clouds and looked down on creation with a knowing, wise, battle-hardened gaze.

Next was the logo. It had to go right in the middle of the cape, which she assumed was valuable and approached me tacitly with an idea that she might keep the cape, to which I agreed. She grabbed some markers, dropped down in front of the TV, and went to work.

Her cousin had already begun her superhero career as Bingo, the Saver Dog. That she is non-canine was never an issue. Never even occurred to me. Of course she's Bingo, the Saver Dog. She drew a dog wearing a cape—on her cape. Voilà, a superhero is born.

But Sarah was more pragmatic and decided that since she was the superhero, she should use her own name. But SARAH is not terribly catchy. It needed punch. It needed pizazz. Obviously, SUPER SARAH. She tried it out. Flew dejectedly around the foyer. It didn't work. It didn't have the—there were any number of Sarahs that could be super. She wasn't unique.

She lands in the living room, leaps onto the couch, cops a stance, and cries out her new name: ABSOLUTELY SUPER SARAH.

Now this was it! This was a name with legs. There could be only one! She was absolute! She dropped down into a hunker before the TV, knocked out her logo—a wonderfully minimal ligature graphic of the initials of her superheroic moniker, Absolutely Super Sarah, in five-inch Sharpie caps—flipped her cape around her shoulders, and rocketed out the front door, down the sidewalk, past all our frail, elderly retired schoolteacher neighbors who couldn't manage poor gerund usage, much less the acronym my absolutely super daughter was sporting on her rippling cape.

For a day, for an afternoon, my girl was a superhero who flew around our hood with A. S. S. written on her back.

F-BOMB REPORT

I should have known something was up. There I sat across from three of Rah's teachers. Like any parent, I was worried. They hadn't told me why I was coming in. They said they'd discuss it when I got there. It could mean only one thing: Rah had done something flagrantly illegal, something mordant and hideous. They were calling me in to dismiss me from parenting forever, then putting her into a "home." Probably with high walls and guards.

I swear there was a single, naked 40-watt bulb over the empty table, and I could barely see their haggard, veteran educator faces. One of them was smoking. They slid my daughter's creative writing essay across the table to me. The room chilled.

I braced myself for the pain and looked across the table expecting a grim visage set in grave concern. I was wrong.

They were smirking.

Teacher: "Mr. Garlington, thank you for joining us."

Me: [pulling a crumpled candy cigarette from my pocket, I puffed a cloud of powdered sugar like nothing's happening] "You make it sound like I had a choice."

Teacher: "Take a look at your daughter's essay and tell me what you see."

I looked down at the paper before me. I glanced. I squinted. I didn't want to show weakness before her teachers—they can smell fear. But as soon as my weary eyes landed on the page I saw a pattern emerge, a carefully laid smattering of code revealed itself, as if my daughter, trapped in her desk in a public school, was trying to send me a message: There, wedged between actual seventh grade vocabulary words, was a string of F-words. A lot of F-words.

She was a sending me a message all right. She was saying, "I am a drunken sailor."

I didn't break. I'm no snitch. I shrugged, worked my candy cigarette to the other side of my mouth and said, "So?" like I was channeling the ghost of Clint Eastwood (Oh come on, *he's dead*; he's been dead since *Gran Torino*).

Or, ok, I actually said, "Well, it's *creative*."

Apparently, this was not the answer they were looking for. They laid into me like grizzled detectives, hammering me with explanations about form and context, about accepted commonalities. They even used the word colloquial. *Colloquial*.

I didn't blink. Because they got nothing on me. I'm a frikkin parent. I'm front line. I know teachers are tough, but when did they ever peel their kids' underwear off the floor or clear a house for lice only to find out it was dandruff? *When have they ever had to fold their daughter's thong?* I've been in the weeds, man.

I held my ground like a rock and . . .

. . . They started laughing.

"Mr. Garlington, we think the essay is a hoot. Seriously, it's the funniest thing we've read in years. Rah is wildly talented."

"Oh, well thank—"

"But she's gonna fail unless you have her change the F-word so the U and the C are replaced by asterisks."

"You're just gonna let me walk out of here?"

"F**K right we are."

THE DOGS

When marrying [My Attorney], there were certain details about her personality and proclivities I was not made aware of. I did not know, for instance, that her entire family was smarter than me and I would spend the next twenty years being trounced in Scrabble, Boggle, Liverpool Rummy, and pretty much everything except poker, which they refuse to play.

Nor did I know about my wife's need to obtain dogs. If I

hadn't made a stand back in the 90s, we'd have a hundred mutts running around our backyard. As it stands, we have three: Whiskey, Tyrone, and James Earl Jones. Whiskey is a stunning little soldier, a pooch of stalwart and steadfast qualities who considers the guardianship of our home his magnum opus and has not stopped barking since we got him. Tyrone, on the other hand, is gay. Being modernists, we embraced his sexuality early on and remain champions of his lifestyle choice.

James Earl Jones is a cat, has been run over by cars twice, and is known in neighborhood as "Killer" for his propensity for birds.

MEET HUMPER, THE WONDER DOG

I love our dog. I love the fact that he's mildly retarded, that he thinks every command means *beg*, that he has an uncanny, nearly supernatural ability to sock me in the balls every time he jumps up into my lap, and that he eats watermelon and popsicles. He is unbearably cute and truly remarkable and I'm going to miss him—but he has to go.

My dog's name is Ty. We got him from a rescue society who found him along the side of the road in Utah. Should've been our first clue. He was damaged goods, harboring a deep wound from his past, nursing a growing neurosis that would one day blossom into an obsession of unrelenting power, a full-blown unmitigated perversion: our dog, that cute little puppy, likes to hump the children.

When I say, "likes to hump the children," I mean that he is ceaselessly driven to stalk unwitting fourth graders and pounce on them the moment they lose a Lego under the couch. The kid bends over and HUMP! Ty is locked on.

It's a sickness, I know, and I ought to just train it out of him, but I think I may have accidentally encouraged his perversion and I feel responsible. See, I had this party and I served some decent scotch, and a buddy of mine, a young comic book writer, thought holding your liquor referred merely to volume and by the end of the party was slumped in the corner of my dining room locked into a slurred scolding of my poor dog, attempting, apparently, to teach Ty to sit.

Ty is untrainable. Although he clearly understands English, he misinterprets everything as being in FRAT dialect.

Sit = Dude!

Beg = Dude!

Roll over = Dude! Dude-Dude!

Play dead = Dude Dude!

*&!!@#$! Idiot dog! = Dude! I love you, dude!

So my buddy finally stands up and declares that he has trained the dog, spins to the right, and staggers into a bedroom where he falls face first onto the bed, his ass in the air like a dirty cartoon. And Ty, who has been in training with the man for the last hour, jumps into bed with him because the bed the man falls into just happens to be the one Ty sleeps in every night. I don't think much of it; I'm just glad the guy finally shut up. A couple of hours later I stop by to do a drunk-check and Ty is going at it like a coke-addled chihuahua on my poor friend who's dead to the world. And here's where I went wrong.

I laughed my ass off. I did. I hung on to the doorjamb and howled while Ty kept going, big stupid dog tongue hanging out, big grin on his snout. Who am I to interfere with true love? So like ten minutes later I kicked him off my friend and locked him in the basement where I'm almost sure he abused the sofa cushions all night.

So a few weeks later my son has a friend over and they're in the basement eviscerating Storm Troopers when I come down with a load of whites and see Roon's friend madly jiggling the controller while the dog's madly jiggling my son's friend.

The kid's pretty much ignoring the dog frottage so he can focus on slaying drones.

"TY! Cut it out!"

The kid glances back at me, still playing, says, "Oh, he does that all the time."

I picture the parade of fourth grade boys who've been hitting the basement game room all summer and suddenly see each and every one of them attacked by my grinning, perverted, horny dog.

I crate Dog Juan and counsel the boys to punch him in the snout next time he tries it. It's a power thing, I tell them, he's just proving who's boss.

Roon doesn't miss a beat: "If that's proving who's boss, I'm never getting a job."

I'M IN A CO-DEPENDENT RELATIONSHIP WITH MY GAY DOG

My dog is gay and he thinks we're married. I'm serious. I've written about my retarded dog previously but just to refresh: My dog is a tardhound and he ain't getting any better.

I noticed it when we first got him from a Border Collie Rescue Mission way out in Idaho. They picked him up on the side of the road and clearly he was busted from square one because his foster masters raised him with cats. When we got him he was house trained and the first time he went out to poop, I noticed that he immediately covered it up. I asked the nice lady who voluntarily drove my dog all the way to Chicago and wouldn't even accept a tip, "Was he . . . was he raised by cats?"

"Oh, a lot of puppies do that. He'll grow out of it."

He still does it. But that doesn't make him gay or retarded, just poop finicky. The retarded part is easily proven by the long list of highly expensive, cherished, or necessary household items he has eaten. Here's a brief excerpt:

My cell phone: $125

My daughter's retainer: $300

My daughter's replacement retainer: $300

A hand-crafted dragon puppet: $120

Half a bag of smuggled whiskey-filled, German chocolate truffles: $15

A hand-carved hunting horn with my great, great, great uncle Lorenzo Garlington's initials carved into it that's been in my family for generations: Priceless.

An Etch a Sketch.

But I can live with (or without) all those things. I got a new cell phone and my daughter's teeth are fine. What's bugging me is how the dog is turning into my gay wife.

Maybe it's because my actual wife, [My Attorney], isn't home that much. Maybe Ty sees an opportunity. Maybe he's just trying to be helpful. I don't know, but the little bastard's nagging me all the time and it's getting on my nerves.

Dog owners, explain this behavior:

He pre-follows me everywhere. He doesn't walk behind me like a real dog, no. He scampers ahead no matter where I'm going, staring at me. I thought at first it might be tracking behavior, maybe a little bloodhound work. But no. The only thing he's tracking is our relationship. He putters ahead of me, his eyes all arched and pleading: "Are you going this way? This way? How about over here? See how much we have in common? I know which way you're going."

It's like we're soul mates.

He comes into whatever room I'm in and instead of lying at my feet with my slippers in his mouth, he stands across the room and stares at me, inching closer and closer, staring: "Is now a good time for petting? How about you pet me now? Now? What about now?"

When I sit down to work, he stands in the middle of the room and stares at me. If I look at him, he'll take a step toward me then back up, sit down, and obviously look away like he wants me to know he knows I don't have any time for him, but he's not going to let me know he knows that. No, he wants me to know he's just perfectly fine. All by himself. Right here. Like three feet from me. Just licking himself, hanging out, don't mind him. La-de-da.

He licks my toes. A lot. I don't ask him to do this and it just weirds me out. I mean the first time it was cute but now it's like all the time and he does it while he's STARING AT ME. I tell him to stop and he steps away then glances back at me like I've hurt his feelings. Like he's saying, "You don't think I'm hot anymore!" It's just twisted.

And don't even get me started about his preference for fourth grade boys.

I know a lot of you see a pattern here and you're thinking a) he needs to pee, or b) he's lonely and just wants some attention. Well, you're wrong. That dog spends more time in my lap than I do. And when he jumps up into my lap, he rolls over on his back, completely heels-to-Jesus, shoves his stupid head up under my chin and moans. Tell me that's not gay.

I had another border collie, Chelsea (R.I.P.), and she did the same kind of things but I chalked it up to her being a bitch and her being fifteen years old. Guy dogs aren't supposed to do that kind of thing, particularly untrained idiotic guy dogs. They're supposed to lie around and lick dirt. They're supposed to crap and sleep and when you call them, they walk over and let you pet them on the head for a minute, then go back to sleep.

You let a regular dog out into the yard and he'll walk right past a burglar, a cat, a rabid barking squirrel, and seven pounds of raw steak, just to crap on the sidewalk then lay down in the shade and start snoring. That's a dog.

My dog leaps into the backyard bark first, his ears all up, prancing—PRANCING!—with his tail in the air like some British office queen shouting, "Now just see here, SEE HERE, you scoundrels! Ruffians! I will NOT tolerate your behavior!" Other dogs walking by are clearly unimpressed, barely managing a canine *whatever* bark. Then he'll run back over to stare at me. I swear his eyebrows are raised. I swear he's all middle management. My dog could work retail: "Can you—did you—My Good Lord, the nerve of that mixed breed terrier to just urinate on the fence like it belonged to him." Stare. Stare. "Well, Sir, are you going to call the cops?"

Damn gay dog.

OF CATS AND MEN

I recently caved to a family request. I feel bad about it. I should have more integrity, more stick-to-my-gunsiness, more guts. Instead, I am a shameless panderer for my children's love. I sold stalwart fortitude for cheap hugs and a fist bump: I let them get a cat.

I've got nothing against cats—don't go Chris Crocker on me here—it's just we live in a small house and I already caved for a second dog, and there might be a third unless that wad of fur struggling to free itself from under the credenza is just a hair ball.

But what's done is done. The cat is here. We've spent the fiscal equivalent of the gross national product of Narnia at Petco, cat-proofed the house, and introduced it to the dogs. Now comes the hard part: naming it.

Most people do that five minutes after getting a pet, but not us—trust me, we tried. But where my integrity crumbles under the whining of my minions, I've drawn a line in the litter box when it comes to a *nom de purr*. I learned my lesson with Dog 2.

We had high hopes for this hound. He had a way of cocking his head and Spocking an eyebrow that made him look like he was solving a Sudoku while learning French. We thought he was a genius. We were wrong.

This dog does not understand the simple universal human/

dog interface of, "Come, Boy." I've sat on the couch with a lapful of fresh bacon, begging him and making hideous kissy noises. Nothing. I'll give up and he'll go chase his own tail. A year and a half and he still does that. Not only does he chase it, he catches it and tries to eat it.

Every.

Day.

But that's not what gives me pause in naming the cat. I'm worried about what the neighbors think.

It took us only a day to name the idiot dog "Whiskey." It's all pirate and rock-n-roll with a just hint of authorial panache. We forgot about the sheer level of pedestrian traffic around our corner lot and what our busy neighbors might think when I lean out the back door in my "I Killed Larry Hagman" T-shirt and ragged pajama pants, my hair attempting escape, holding a coffee cup like I'm begging for change, yelling, "WHISKEY! WHISKEY, WHIIIISKEY!"

People shield their children and speed up.

My short list of acceptable cat names include but are not limited to: "Top of the morning," "Have a nice day," and "Please don't be alarmed, everything is going to be fine." My kids don't care. They named him regardless of what I think and, because they are cruel, malicious, and apparently patricidal, here's what I'll be yelling out the door next time we accidently let him out:

"Luke, I am your father."

SQUIRT BOTTLE POLITICS

A squirt bottle is my new best friend.

I ought to elaborate here. Last year we tried to train our dogs to stop licking everything on earth by hiring a trainer. They licked her face the entire visit, which she refused to acknowledge. She said that if she acknowledged the licking, the dogs would keep licking her. I thought perhaps I could employ dog whisperer techniques I'd learned from watching reality TV:

"But he's still licking you," I whispered.

"Eventually he'll stop," she whispered back.

"But I want him to stop now," I rasped.

"You just have to ignore him," she said as my dog curled his tongue up her left nostril and out her ear.

She went on to deliver poorly rehearsed instructions on how to use a squirt bottle and held out her hand for the eight hundred bucks we owed her. I just stood there. My wife told me to write her a check.

"Just ignore her and she'll stop," I whispered.

She left us with our dogs licking the TV as we stared at our $800 squirt bottle.

The instructions for the squirt bottle are complicated and involve dog trainer jargon that I will try to summarize for you, gentle reader:

Point. Squirt. Repeat.

Kind of like shampoo, but instead of wild hibiscus, your living room ends up smelling like wet border collie.

And it doesn't work—on dogs. It works miraculously on children.

AN OPEN LETTER FROM MY DOGS

Dear Bipeds:

We are concerned. As practicing members of the canine subculture, we dogs face a constant problem of dehydration. It is vital to us that we are provided with adequate water at all times.

By adequate, we mean, of course, clean. To that point, we need to address certain habits of the uprights that have come to our attention.

Firstly, allow me to say, and I'm speaking for myself and the short one who tries to hump me all the time, we have deep and abiding respect for you and all the two-legs in the house. As you know, we are in the habit of licking you on a fairly regular basis. This is our way of showing you our respect and affection (albeit, we're also checking for pizza crumbs). We are, in the humblest manner, as they say in the street, your dogs (YO!).

Secondly, we feel compelled to bring to your attention your usage of the water bowl located in the bathroom. Although you do a remarkable job keeping this bowl full of fresh, clean water, free of debris, and available to us quadrupeds, you also seem to enjoy urinating in it. Regularly.

Suffice it to say, we're displeased. We drink out of that bowl, good sirs. We dip our unprotected snouts in that water several times each day and we do so with a certain mindlessness that comes from habitual behavior (I assume you've read Pavlov and Skinner—you know how this works), i.e., we don't check first. We just start lapping, and to do so and suddenly realize one of the vertical kind has marked the bowl again is, well—"surprising" would be diplomatic.

We're not asking for much and we know this is a cultural difference that needs to be addressed with care, but could you possibly start urinating outdoors like a good dog? Peeing in our water bowl is just rude and leads to aggressive behavior (I don't want to sound threatening, but have you looked in your shoes today?).

In closing, if you could please find it in your heart to reform this unacceptable habit, we'll stop peeing on the couch.

With warmest regards,

The Dogs

THE HORROR

And now we come to the core of my parenting nightmare. These are the parts of parenting Dr. Spock didn't tell you about. These are the chapters missing from every advice book ever written. These are the episodes that foster serious regret at having spawned, the episodes that remind you if you hadn't procreated, you'd be sipping sauternes on the Seine right now instead of being elbow deep in the macabre garrison of parenthood.

LICE, LICE BABY!

Nothing makes a parent feel more like a degenerate knuckle-sucking bat-shit crazy shut-in than finding lice on their kid's head.

When I was a child, I lived in rural Alabama. Took the bus to school. I lived in a decent part of the county, good people, lots of churches, good soil. But there were pockets of insanity that can only happen when people are deeply isolated from public transportation and cable TV. The trailer kids, for instance.

My bus would stop at the trailer kids' place, which was a dirty white single-wide set about a football field back off the main highway at the end of a weed-choked, puddle-pocked red dirt driveway. It was never quite level and the door was gone. In the two years I rode the bus to school, that trailer never had a door. The kids would be standing at the side of the highway in perfectly starched shirts, perfectly pressed pants, lunchboxes in hand, their faces poking out through a pale circle of clean. It was incongruous and weird and to this day the open door of that trailer is like the drooling maw of Hell in my head.

When I found a fully adult louse crawling through my son's head, my whole house morphed into that crooked, doorless tornado target. I was disgusted. I wanted to move.

You read the lice notices from school and you secretly smirk and think, "God, which aborigine kid is this about?" And wallow in the self-satisfied luxury of knowing it ain't yours. Until it is.

I'd hunted for lice before. I'd held a promising dandruff flake under the magnifying glass with my wife leaning over my shoulder, laptop open to a Googled image of a bug zoomed to Cthulian proportions. But we'd never found one. We just spent a lot of time tsking at the parents of children with lice, all black-tie ball and fund raiser, champagne glass to our lips, asking in a nervous whisper, "You think it was the Greenburgs' kids?"

But no. It was my kids wearing a lice wig. And I had to make the call to the school and I realized that even if every other parent in the school didn't get a note saying, BEWARE THE FAMILY G FOR THEY ARE BESOT WITH VERMIN, the frikkin receptionist knows. Might as well wear a sandwich board.

So I buy enough chemicals to qualify as a superfund site, and dunk Roon's head into a bucket of foul smelling gunk and carefully pull the NIT COMB through his hair and inspect it under the glass after every pull. My wife, who used to be an industrial hygienist, has gone into hazmat mode. She's full-on FEMA. She announces we have to wash all the sheets and blankets.

All. Of. Them.

Everyone takes their special bath and does the monkey grooming daisy chain, and we stay up till 3 a.m. washing bed linens until we're reasonably certain the lice are dead. We wait three days and do it again because the eggs we missed might've hatched. We refuse all phone calls and don't go anywhere. We might as well be quarantined with a great big crimson L stitched on our chests.

So I send the kid to school with a note explaining our

multifaceted assault on the infestation. They call me to take him home. He still has lice.

I stick him under a lamp and get the glass and there, behind his ear—eggs. Worse, as I'm looking at the eggs, an adult louse wiggles out from behind a hair. Let me tell you, these things are not hard to see. It was like a rhinoceros. I actually smacked it and Roon yelped. So we do another day of treatment. I send him to school. They send him back.

I buy another truckload of chemicals. I spray the mattresses, the couch, the love seat, wash ALL of his clothes, spray his drawers, spray the dog, throw away his baseball hats, tuques, combs. I throw away all our brushes, buy more at the dollar store, get another bottle of VILE FOUL LICE KILLING PASTE and slather all our heads like I'm laying brick. Me and [My Attorney] seriously consider shaving our heads and having the house fumigated. Another mom happens to call us to see if Roon has chicken pox because if he does, she wants her kids to get it and get the whole chicken pox thing over with. I admit the dark truth. She cracks up: "Yeah, us too." She says her kids had it but they killed 'em with mayonnaise.

Mayon—*naise*?

Mayonnaise. Hellman's to be precise, because when you bring out the Hellman's, you bring out the best. We put a chair in the middle of the kitchen and got some shower caps and to prove it wasn't entirely bizarre, I went first. Let the kids dope my head an inch deep. I smelled like a hoagie for an hour, but I have to say, after shampooing it something like thirty times, my hair felt luxuriously thick and manageable.

So we send the kid to school the next day and he sticks. We do the sandwich head trick three days later much to everyone's hilarity, and we've been lice free ever since.

OLD SUPERMAN

As a stay-at-home mom/dad, I'm accustomed to finding myself in situations dripping with gender role–reversal irony. I wear an apron, I cook casseroles, I cry at that Sylvan commercial with the skateboard and the music and the grades. I can talk to my daughter's gynecologist without stabbing myself in the eyes.

I chuckle at these Mr. Mom moments. I'm still all man. I smoke cigars. I scratch. But when I see the new young dads hugged by their mini-me's, I cry like a princess because I want a baby and that has me acting weird.

Weird like I'm not leaving my house weird. My neighborhood is swarming with brand new stay-at-home dads and their hyper-adorable baby boys. Every seven seconds, one of those mop-haired little dynamos flings himself into the open arms of his beaming pop, yelling, "I love you, man!" And I start crying.

I have to be careful because my wife is going through withdrawal and wants another baby and she can afford to get one without me. The only thing keeping her from adopting a Nigerian war baby is my (apparent) insouciant indifference, but if she catches me sobbing in the bay window as some thirty-something noob tousles his boy's hair, she'll be on a plane stat.

I thought it might be hormonal, so I went to my doctor.

Dr.: "Do you have ovaries?"

Me: "Not on me."

Dr.: "So, it's not hormonal. Let me try something." [He cues up the opening scene from The Andy Griffith Show.]

Me: "I [weep] want [weep] a [weep] bay-hay-bee!" [uncontrollable weeping]

Dr.: "When was the last time your son hugged you?"

Me: [sniff] "Voluntarily?"

Dr.: "Oh, good lord."

And that's it. That's what's wrong with me. I don't have this problem with the girl—she's hug-centric. I have to peel her off me every fourteen seconds. But my son has turned into a pre-man. He used to wear his emotions like a dirty SpongeBob T-shirt. Now he keeps them buried under his professional grade video game skill set and music snobbery. He used to leap into my arms. Now he high-fives me.

Sometimes.

If my calculations are correct, I've only got a precious handful of embraces left:

1. When (if) he graduates.

2. When (if) he gets married.

3. His son's first F-bomb.

4. As I lay dying (maybe).

I know what this is. I know how it works. It's not my hormones that are the problem, it's his. He's got hair on his lip.

He eats like a horse. He smells like a mule. He's watches Colbert. He's in the short stretch to manhood. Suddenly, he's not seeing me as the Superman he thought I was when he was five. He's seeing me as the feeble, addled, wild-haired, unshaven dork in a stained T-shirt I actually am.

That's why I'm crying every time I peep over the window ledge at those bright, sparkling newbie dads.

Their boys still see them as heroes and, more importantly, they still believe it's true. I miss that self-deception. It fuels all the idiotic crap we do as dads (camping, ice fishing, parking lot doughnuts), and it's a blast. For that brief crazy handful of years, we're invincible. We're hilarious. We're awesome.

Now, as he grabs my wallet out of my hand on his way (to an undisclosed secret teen lair), it's clear I have no one left to be an idiot for. I will wither up and blow away and that is, perhaps, why I've become pathetic and weepy.

My kids, they're my kryptonite, and for a while, a long time ago, I was their Superman.

DEVELOPING A DADFACE

I want to talk to the fathers today. Especially the new guys. Hi. Welcome.

Google tells me there are close to 2.2 million of you staying at home, raising your kids, and doing work the last generation reserved for people with vaginas. Now you find yourself in a job for which there are three bajillion handy blogs giving you advice, all of it wrong.

I'm not a new guy. I'm an old guy. I come from a generation that saw the installation of colored tee-vees. Our morning cartoons were interrupted by Watergate. We're grizzled and haggard and worn down and we're here to tell you something: You're doing it wrong.

You are gentle and firm and worthy of admiration and I appreciate it, I do, but in your overhauling of the good dad toolbox, you've discarded a tool you really, really need. You need a Dadface.

That thing you see in the mirror? That is the face of a dad, but it is not a Dadface. You know the Dadface. Your dad had one, remember? There you are on your skateboard ramp using his $300 seven-iron for ramp jousting. He comes out of nowhere and doesn't say a word. He just stares. Like Magneto with a three-day beard, he uses only the power of his splenetic visage, bending you to his will, causing you to carry that seven-iron over to him in perfect silence, your pancreas withering in his gaze.

He didn't need to yell. He didn't need to hit. He only had to stare. No violence. No bruises. No therapy.

You tried it. Your kid races into the playground fountain with his shoes and socks on and you think, "This is it. I'm using the stare!" You turn your grim countenance toward your child who promptly falls into a slump of giggling oh-my-gods because you look like you just pooped your shorts and here, here my friend, is where you've failed.

It isn't about the way the dad's face appears. Your pop didn't make a face. His face was perfectly blank. No furrowed brow. No jutting chin. Nothing. A purely blank emotionless mug. Yet you felt your liver clench. It's not about the facial expression. There is no facial expression. It's about what's in your heart and I'm telling you, newbie, for a proper Dadface, you have to fill your heart with a dark inflexible vengeance. You have to suffuse your soul with a murderous spirit. You have to truly believe, while watching your progeny pee in the front yard on a Sunday: *I will kill him*.

Don't tell me that emotion doesn't flit past. I know. I've spent the last fifteen years planning my son's horrific death. I know. It's there. Don't feel bad, it's natural. We're programmed to feel this way. We are, thankfully, civilized enough to resist the urge. Because we love our children, we do. We adore them.

Remember when your son said *&^%$# in front of your posse and you all fell down laughing? That's a good feeling. That's bonding.

Remember when he said it in front of your in-laws then turned and looked at you? That's a Dadface feeling.

THE FAMILY BRAAAP

I didn't marry my wife because she can burp the alphabet, but it was right up there with being hot and wicked smart. However, when my kids asked me why I married her (with a little too much of a "What the hell were you thinking?!" in their voice...), I gave them the alphaburp spiel.

She can do it, too. My wife's ability to brap alphabetically is impressive and worthy of video (we have not—yet), but lately she won't do it. She won't pony up. My son will get down on his knees but she won't crack. She's a lawyer now and that kind of behavior won't hunt.

But the two or three times she broke it out for the kids forever changed their idea of burping. For most kids, a good fricative FRAAAP will do. But not ours. Our kids have goals.

The princess gave up early. It doesn't please the court. She gets to about J then loses focus. But the kid, he's committed.

My wife taught him how to fake burp in order to get through all twenty-six letters. She neglected to explain the physics involved: When you swallow a lot of air, it kind of makes you a human balloon and the air...it needs to come out.

So one day Roon is working it. He's horfing air like a Hoover and pumping out magnificently phlegmatic ligatures but he can't get past M without cracking up. So he's working on his game face when he fades. Just peters out. He wanders into the bathroom and sits down on the edge of the tub.

I'm on the phone (I don't recall the conversation but given the sheer idiotic guyness of coaching my son to better burping, more than likely there were a lot of *Dudes!* and air-fives) when I notice Roon is gripping the edge of the sink and staring at the floor with a look that either means, "I'm giving birth," or "This happened in *Alien*." Then he screams.

My son is scared of spiders—and there's one chick on his basketball team that railroads him to the hoop like a freaking bulldozer and he just stands there blinking—so I'm not saying he's tough. But when it comes to puking, diarrhea, and any other ungainly expectorations, he's a pro. No prob. If he has to puke, he pauses the DVR, says, "Pardon, methinks I must hurl, forthwith," hits the can, cleans up, and returns to SpongeBob like nothing happened.

If you didn't catch it previously, I don't freak out. I don't call 911. I don't scare easily. So when *mon fils* started wailing and wouldn't stop, when his screaming started getting louder, harder, more urgent, I grabbed the phone.

I've never felt so useless and stupid—staring at Roon, patting him on the back, the arms, not knowing what the hell is going on, and thinking his stomach is knotted, his heart decavitating, his spleen exploding, and he's looking at me like I'm supposed to know what's going on. I ask him what's wrong and he nails me, his face contorted with horror and surprise: "Don't you know?"

The paramedics burst through the door and the street fills

up with sirens and red lights and they hit the hallway, all radios, faceplates, and gear, and Roon looks up, astonished, revelation dawning, and he burps.

For thirty-eight seconds.

It is a luxurious, arresting, and august irruption. It is a venting of such sepulchral weirdness it seems to disrupt the natural order: Birds fall from the sky, wolves howl, Republicans forgive someone, and time stops, yet the burp just keeps coming, just keeps unraveling like a magic act, and even Roon, in the middle of it, starts to laugh while he's belching. I'm laughing. The paramedics sitting at my kitchen table are cracking up. Roon, giggling, continues to erupt: short, echoing bursts of FRAAAP and CRARRRG and BLAAAAGH—like Batman for blind people.

The paramedics advise us to administer a folk remedy: Coke. Burp boy keeps up his vaporous ellipses. The bleats get further apart and stop catching him by surprise and before the paramedics leave, he manages one last massive BLAAAAP!

He uses it to say *thank you*.

PINEWOOD DERPY

Let us establish now that I am not very good at this fatherhood thing. Never have been, never will be. I am a struggling father, an amateur, a dilettante. My children know this—I've been proving it to them since they were born. For my son, the proof was never so obvious as during the Pinewood Derby.

I tend to plan the way some people fall off a cliff. I back plan, coming to my senses moments after something expensive lies smoldering at my feet long enough to say, "Maybe I should have read the instructions." I also tend to reject proper tool usage to the point where Menard's has issued a restraining order.

So nobody should be surprised I screwed up my Pinewood Derby car.

So nobody should be surprised I screwed up my son's Pinewood Derby car.

First of all, the manufacturer's verbiage claiming their paint will dry in one hour is a big fat lie. The only thing happening in an hour is the Scoutmaster will come into the broom closet where you're building your car (your son's car) AS THE DERBY IS STARTING to tell you [unprintable] or he will [unprintable]. And the wheels will get stuck to the fuselage.

Which really doesn't matter in the great story arc of life. But there is a moment when it does matter. There is, in fact, a moment when those wheels, shellacked to the body of the car by a generous application of Krylon Red #5, bear the weight of a '57 Chevy in a single glance, as your son tries to place his racecar on the track . . . and it sticks to his fingers.

However, there is another moment even heavier. When the chucks release and all the cars speed down the slope toward the finish line. All the cars.

Except his.

Yeah, the manufacturer coulda said something about that.

Look, I know something about being shamefaced: I attempted dating in the 80s. I worked at a theme park. I drove a Gremlin. I drove a purple Gremlin.

So I knew how to react. I knew precisely the harrowing precipice of dignity my father-and-son dynamic skidded uncontrollably toward in the gravity of that glance. As my son's public humiliation went nuclear, as an entire auditorium of parents shushed, their heads swiveling in unison toward me, as the raw force of an accumulated scowl swept toward me like a bright red tsunami, I thought to myself: "I should have used a hair dryer."

The next year was no better. Heck, the next two years were no better. My car—my son's car—never placed. I spent at least fifty bucks on kits, sand paper packs, chrome pipes, and high gloss lacquer. But no matter how many hours I put into my car—into my son's car—I didn't place. He didn't place.

Finally the kid said, "Dad, can I try?" and then I got it. I mean, it was soooo obvious. I should have seen it coming a mile away: This was one of those blunt lessons of fatherhood, a Zen smack, a light bulb as bright as the sun, and it was shining across that dim auditorium directly onto me and I knew, I knew right then. I needed powdered graphite lube.

The kid was having none of it. He grabbed a chunk of pine and built what appeared to be a wedge of cheese with a number 7 scrawled on its side. It wasn't sanded. The wheels were crooked. It was yellow. This car had nothing going for it.

He didn't win. I mean, he was racing a block of cheddar against a SpongeBob, a third-generation doorstop, and a perfectly rendered 1967 Camaro Super Sport. He came in fourth.

And he didn't care.

Winning had nothing to do with it.

Winning has nothing to do with it.

FONDLY FOND OF FONDLING THE FAMILY JEWELS!

It's a man thing. It's unavoidable. We can't help it: God designed us so that our hands fall in our lap and, well, since they're there, we figure we ought to use them for something cause we're all about practicality and getting her done, and *ergo sphericum* we scratch.

Sometimes we don't even itch. In fact, I'd have to say in this day and age of soap and instant hot showers and excellent laundry services and all the other things that separate us from the Amish and the eighteenth century, we rarely have any real reason to claw the baubles save one: it reasserts our manhood.

My daughter doesn't buy it, however. In fact, if I scratch myself in front of her one more time she might stab me with her iPod.

It's not like I plan this. I don't have an Outlook reminder that says, "8:47 a.m. Scratch balls." It's unconscious. It's like a tic.

But tell that to my daughter.

This morning I walked out into the living room where she's waiting for the limo to take her to school and it's picture day so she's dressed like a rock star. I mean she looks stunning: black silk dress, choker, diamond earrings, and an unnaturally prominent display of boobage. I'm wearing a modified wife-beater

T-shirt, Jack Daniels jams, and my head looks like it's being humped by a drug-addled squirrel. Then I hustle the boys.

"Daaaaaaaaaaaad! God! GOD! What's your PROBLEM! Do you have to do that in front of me EVERY TIME?!"

"IT'S A REFLEX!"

"I don't care! Stop it!"

"OK," scritch scritch.

"DAD!"

"D'oh!"

"Don't be such a man!"

"Sorry."

"Now go get my black strapless bra."

I swear this is verbatim.

PUKEZILLA ATTACKS

My wife's first job involved testing water. It often found her flung to the remotest regions of Florida horse country, which is how I ended up in a hotel room with my infant daughter watching bad movies and bitching to myself.

Since she got per diem and a hotel room, we'd turn her jobs into mini vacations. Occasionally a job would land her in Miami or Fort La-de-da, which were always luxurious and ended with us staggering back to our hotel room at 3 a.m. exuberantly inebriated (therefore: children). But most jobs had her working an abandoned gas station where walking the baby involved diesel fumes and broken glass.

So there I am, watching *A-Team* reruns while Rah is rolling around on the bed. She can't even sit up yet. She's new and fragile, like highly animated pudding. I have no idea what to do with her. I make faces, cute noises. All I get is disdain and dirty diapers.

Around the time Mr. T is welding giant teeth on a golf cart, Rah starts grousing. The grouse turns into a kind of rarified staccato, like someone trying to jump start a Dr. Seuss car, then escalates into full-blown screaming horror. Her little face is crimson. She's squirming to beat hell. And I'm deeply panicked. It's the kind of stupid fear confusion that makes a guy put on one shoe, a hat, and no pants before running out into the parking lot to jump up and down, scream-crying, "Somebody call 911." Not me. I didn't do that. Hell, I'd write about it if I did.

So I'm in this hotel room (not in the parking lot, pantsless, jumping up and down scream-crying) with *l'enfant hole shite* when suddenly she stops. She stops and she stares at me and her eyes start to widen.

Now imagine this part in slowmo.

I pick her up, my hands under her arms, and I get real close because I think that since she stopped screaming that things have gotten even worse, that something inside her, something internal, has gone horribly wrong. Before I can blink, she opens her mouth and horfs in my face.

When I say horf, I want you to understand we're not talking a little tartar sauce on the shoulder. We're talking serious fluid dispersion. Hurlcane Katrina.

You ever see those nature shows where they're filming the seashore and the ocean, like the entire ocean, pounds itself through a tiny hole in a rock and spews foam thirty feet in the air and knocks live birds out of the sky and sinks ships? It was like that, only chunky.

Sure, I saw it coming, but I was holding her—what could I do?! I managed to wang my head sideways to avoid the initial sluice but Rah had morphed into Pukezilla and there was no avoiding it. Against the known laws of physics, she had a limitless supply of fetid, lactatious effluvium and—again, we're in slowmo here—*was trying to see it as it came out of her*. She'd never hurled so she was checking it out, or trying to, but as she'd cock her head to dig the unending jet cascading out of her mouth it would whip around like a psychotic cobra. She's squirming, craning her neck, trying to take it all in as she gets it all out. She was an Exorcist-level, 360-degree, panoramic vomit volcano.

I can't put her down because I think she might choke and I can't turn her away because I've been slimed and I can barely hold on—I'm afraid I'll drop her—so I just take it. Head to toe.

I'm not such a wimp anymore. If this happened now, after dropping both my kids more than once, after seeing them drive their foreheads, temples, jaws, eyeballs, and nearly every other soft part of them into various corners, mortises, baseball bats, pocket knives, handlebars, terrazzo floors, and each other, and still get As in math, I'm a little less likely to give a crap if they fall down. Now if Rah yells, "I hurt myself!" from the basement, my first response is, "Are you bleeding yet?" If Pukezilla attacked now, I'd toss her slimy ass on the bed and take a shower.

So she finally finishes. The bed is a foamy lake of alabaster chum. There's a trail of it across the floor, across the TV, and splattering the lampshade. I look like someone dumped a barrel of cottage cheese over my head.

I look down at my Pukezilla, who's squirming again, and I expect another gusher. I resign myself to a life covered in goo. I set my jaw and steel my demeanor.

She's laughing.

Not giggling. Not chuckling. She's shaking with unalloyed, from the toes, "look at you, you horf-covered dick" guffaws.

Thirteen years later, she still thinks it's funny.

DEATH BY KITTY

Allow me to just come out at the front of this thing and tell you that I do not like cats. I'm not some weirdo militant cat torturer or anything, it's just that in my house there's room for exactly one distant, disaffected, lazy animal, and that spot's been filled (*nice to meet you*). You'll read in the next couple of graphs about our cat dying and you might detect a certain lack of emotion from your humble scribe. Go ahead and hate me: I don't miss her much. This post is not about the dead cat. It's about my live kids and how they handled it and how a parent needs to trust their kids to be resilient and strong. The cat? *What cat?*

While Darth was away in Delaware arguing the validity of ferret slang, our beloved (by three of four) kitty, Share (pronounced shar-RAY), started losing weight by the minute, hid under our bed, and stopped eating. We took her to our vet thinking maybe she had a virus, but we learned instead that she had one of those bizarre semi-genetic kitty cancers and it had grown into her stomach. My wife called me from the vet while I was picking up the kids and told me the sorry news: Share probably wouldn't make it through the next hour.

Meanwhile, my daughter's dress rehearsal for her lead in *Annie Jr.* was scheduled for after school. My daughter, calm, cool, and super pro as always, was sailing through the play prep with aplomb. But she loves her cat. When I say her cat, let me tell you: This was one female feline. Share slept at Rah's feet. She cried when Rah wasn't home. They were connected. So I had a dilemma.

Should I tell her right then?

It's a tough question because I'm all about full disclosure. My son asked me what libido meant the other day and I told him. While he was eating an egg roll. I had to scrape it off the wall.

But my daughter's professionalism would go out the window at the news of her kitty's impending demise. The whole play depended on her, an entire school having worked tirelessly for weeks to put on their first musical in something like eighty years. She was the carter-pin for the whole thing. She's in every scene. Freak her out and the entire production stops.

Because she is good. And when I say good, I'm talking future full of limos good. I'm talking *American Idol* winner good. I'm talking Britney Spears ass-flattening, kick-ass good. I'm talking look for her name in lights soon good.

I called the school. I asked for the music teacher, my daughter's biggest fan, and told her—and she went Montessori on me: Don't tell her. Please wait.

So I did.

I knew it meant her kitty might croak before she had a chance to say goodbye and I knew that Rah would not forgive me for it. But I felt there was a responsibility to the other kids and teachers, adjunct staff, volunteers, janitors, principals, parents, and the other seven hundred thousand people it took to get this thing off the ground.

Rah walked out of the school on top of the world. She floated out of the school. She was three feet off the ground. Not only had the dress rehearsal been a tremendous success, the local paper had interviewed and photographed my daughter, directing the limelight like a blinding nuclear flash into her eyes. Then she hopped into the car and I dropped a bomb on her. I might as well have punched her in the face.

She didn't take it well. I felt horrible. She plummeted from cloud nine to the seventh circle of hell, bounced, and drug her soul across the rocks and cried hard. We drove to the vet, our dear friend Lady D, who showed the kids the x-ray of Share, which looked like the cat had swallowed a football. She was cancer and cat. She was quiet and still and breathing with difficulty, and my kids held her and cried like soldiers and said goodbye.

Rah was particularly strong about it. She talked to the cat and sang to her and I had to take my cynical self and stuff it in a hole and absorb this. It was a critical moment, an unfunny moment, a moment that was engraving itself into my children's minds right before my very eyes. I had to handle it carefully and I think I did. I was hands off about it. I facilitated tissues and hugs, trips to the bathroom, counsel with the vet, and kept my mouth shut. I explained things quietly and succinctly without my usual pedantic lecturing and over explaining. I respected their hearts.

I was proud of them for their powerful grief. I know that sounds weird, but not everyone—not even every kid—is capable of real grief. I guess I should say that I was proud of the power of their grieving. It was unabashed. It was without artifice whatsoever. It was noble.

So we drove home while Darth did the dirty work (she is a lawyer). I felt like I needed to steer their grief toward mirth and so I turned to our most powerful tool: television. We turned on *American Idol* and Sanjay's faux-hawk was waggling on camera and we all cracked up instantly. I served ice cream and we made jokes and watched the Simpsons and the grief tapered off.

Like any parent, I was afraid of the grief. I hated to see my kids go through the pain of it, the fear of it, the intensity. I knew what it was like—I'd had a favorite dog killed by a truck when I was young and it was terrifying. And I know parents who try to soften it with euphemisms, delays, and outright deceit. I chose the path of honesty (albeit delayed by two hours for the sake of the play) and trusted my monkeys to handle it. And yes they grieved hard, they hurt, they were deeply affected and powerfully sad. But it was good. It was proper.

I kept my own secret relief, which I know is evil and perverse, to myself. I was consoling my kids, but in my mind I was thinking about who would inherit the $300 robotic cat box and how fast I could get rid of it.

The next morning, I dropped off my son and he could barely rocket out of the car fast enough. All that crying and heaving and sobbing and he tumbled out of the Camry yelling at his friend: "Dude! We put our cat to sleep! It's totally dead!"

American Idol and ice cream: the balm of patriots.

SCREAMING TO YOUR KIDS ABOUT SEX

All parents dread this moment. You notice the hairy legs. (I'm talking about your son.) You hear the voice crack. You race out to buy deodorant by the gallon. All of a sudden, you realize: it's deep in the sticky wicket of puberty. So you—out of duty, out of a misguided sense of tradition, because you think you care—decide to have a talk. The talk.

Let me offer you a word of advice for parents of the post-Google pubescent:

Don't. Talk. About. Sex.

They know more than you do. They're like obsessed ob-gyn scientists. My thirteen-year-old son has probably seen more pictures of the va-jay-jay than I have in my entire life. If, like me, you are a highly liberal parent and don't squelch the Internet, then the first time you talk to your kid about sex, you are doomed to feel like a shy Amish farm boy dropped into a pool full of Vaseline and naked Brazilian trannies.

To wit:

Dad: "Son, I think I need to talk to you about sex."

Son: "Cool, Dad. What do you want to know?"

Dad: "No, I mean, I'm here to answer any questions you might have.

Son: "Oh good, because I was curious about a few things." [pulls a ream of paper from his desk drawer] "Do you and mom ever [I TUNE IT OUT BY SCREAMING IN MY HEAD: AAAAAAAAA!]?"

Dad: "Dear god."

Son: "So that's a 'no.' Is it because you're afraid your [AAAAAAA!] will [AAAAA!] or that your [AAAAA!] isn't [AAAA!] enough?"

Dad: "Mother of Christ."

Son: "Also, when girls say they're willing to [AAAAAAAAAA!], do they really mean they'll [AAAAA!] or that they just want to cuddle?"

Dad: "Didn't I give you a pocket knife when you were ten?"

Son: "Why?"

Dad: "I need to cut my throat."

Son: "Don't be such a prude. Now, here's a picture of two people [AAAAAAA! AAAAA!] in a room full of [AAAAAAA!] in Turkey, and what I'm wondering is, in other cultures, is it normal for a spectator at such an event to [AAAAAA!] with his [AAAAAA!] in a tea pot?"

Dad: "I'm gonna throw up."

Son: "Also, sometimes when I [AAAAAAAAAAAAAAAAA!] I think about [AAAAAAAAAAA AAAAAAAAAAAA!]. Is that normal?"

Dad: "NO! Oh my GOD! NO! Stop!"

Son: "Finally, have you ever [MOTHER OF ALL THINGS HOLY,

THAT IS NOT AN ACCEPTABLE THING TO HEAR, EVER, NOT EVEN IN A MERCHANT MARINE SHIP'S BRIG AFTER A FIGHT. MY GOD!], and did you get a rash?"

Dad: "Please stop talking. Please—"

Son: "Is this normal?" [Shows photograph of AAAAAAAAAA AAAAAAAA!]

Dad: "I'll do anything. Anything."

Son: "Can I get a new game dedicated desktop with nine terabytes of RAM and an oil-cooled hard drive?"

Dad: "Here's my credit card."

As I leave the room, he calls his friend and I hear:

"Mission accomplished."

FULL MOON OVER WISCONSIN DELLS

We went to the Dells. Growing up in Florida, we had a lot of cool natural stuff to enjoy—rivers, lakes, Disney—and we had beaches. A lot of them. No matter where you are in Florida, you're never more than an hour and a half from the beach. So in my childhood memory box are sweaty trips down the Bee-line (that's a highway, not a train) to New Smyrna and Daytona Beach.

But in all my years there, I never learned to surf. Believe it or not, people in Florida surf. You don't get the same kind of waves they get in Cali or Hawaii, for the love of God, but you can catch a wave and stand up and do some tricks before you run over the pale people of Michigan standing in the shallows looking for sharks.

I did learn to body surf, which is a remarkable skill for a fat guy. I can jump in the face of a wave and ride it in and let me tell you, it's a very cool feeling and I can only assume it's twice as cool on a surfboard.

And being a teen in the Land of Lakes and Daytona, I can tell you stories of women losing their tops in the waves or behind a ski-boat, it's happened millions of times. How many people do we know who've dived into a pool only to leave their shorts on the surface with their pride? But it's never happened to me.

Until the Dells.

Our son, The Finagler, finagled his way into the vacation plans of some close friends who were visiting a Ukrainian Youth Camp in Baraboo, Wisconsin. A Ukrainian Youth Camp is a clapboard motel refurbished only enough so that live snakes and bears can't actually reach through the walls to eat you. It is not the height of luxury. My son went there and a few days later, we booked a room twenty miles north in the Dells, picked him up from youth camp, and took off.

In the days preceding that, my son had gone to a place called Noah's Ark, which is water-park heaven, and lost his water-park cherry. He had grown fierce and brave and determined to find a slide, somewhere, that was actually vertical and hopefully deposited riders into the open air a half mile over a shark infested vat of radioactive yak vomit.

We booked a hotel that included the world's largest indoor water park and when we gazed upon it's polycarbonate glory, my son punched me in the arm and demanded that I ride every slide with him, to which I acquiesced and then puked into a garbage can.

The first slide we go on is called the Man-Eating-Blade-Choked-Maw-of-Death-Python and like most of the slides is an enclosed tube modeled somewhat on the lower intestines in which you are voluntarily flushed into a small pool whereupon you crack your skull on the cement berm at the far side. The tube has seventy-five turns and a hundred and thirty-one drops and it lies somewhere between eighty-eight and ninety degrees of vertical so at some points you're not sliding so much as falling feet first in total darkness with nothing but the sound of your own scream—but it's ok because it only lasts about forty-five minutes.

To get to the beginning of these slides, you walk up forty-four flights of stairs, the elbows of the slides resting just inches away so that every time a body slams into the turn, you can feel the concussion like a piano dropped off the back porch. So it's great. After throwing yourself down "The Well," which is an unlighted vertical pit with rocks and dead bodies at the bottom, and getting your heart rate up to three hundred beats per minute, you then have to carry a three-ton raft back up all six hundred and thirty-one flights of stairs. I finally threw myself off the top to commit touristocide, but landed in some guy's commemorative Mai Tai and survived.

Once we'd exhausted the terrifying outdoor slides, we went to the indoor park for the terrifying indoor slides, and as we walked in, we noticed there was a standing wave. You stand at the top and simply drop in. It was far too cool to pass up AND had the benefit of only being about ten feet tall and SLOPED, so not only were there no dark turns, I could slip down the thing and survive. We stood in line and watched the Wisconsin lifeguard/super jock/surf Nazis do their little hot dog routines to impress the girls. They flipped, spun, rolled, and finally fell down the front of the wave, rolling headfirst into a flip, out of which they simply walked up to the nearest blushing girl-will-go-wild like they'd just stepped out of their dorm. I figured if a perfectly buff nineteen-year-old hotshot farm boy can do it, so can I.

So my son's turn came and he was surprisingly adroit, staying up on his "board" and having a blast before he fell off and was blasted back up to the landing area. Then my turn came.

I know from my writing you probably think I'm some George

Clooney–Matt Damon double and thanks for the compliments, and the flowers, really. But truth is, I'm slightly overweight. And hairy. And by slightly overweight, I mean it looks like I might give birth to a fully grown wildebeest at any moment, and by hairy I mean I can braid the hair on my back. *From my front.* And I don't tan well. Furthermore, I'd like to say that I'm bringing sexy back. Mostly because it looks like a miniature orange Speedo on me.

So I drop in from the top, half expecting the thing to shut down and management to come out and have a talk with me but, amazingly, I glide down the face of this wave with real grace and panache and then I kind of hang there in the middle, just like you're supposed to, surfing. My inner nine-year old retarded sociopath takes the controls and convinces me to try to skim from side to side like the surf jockeys were doing, so I lift the edge of my raft and it throws me off into the 300 mph wave and eats my pants.

Now, in a lake, if you lose you shorts, you can stand there and try to get the attention of your friends and hope to God they'll help you out. Even in a pool you can stand in the deep end and beg someone to throw you a towel. But the standing wave water that shoots out of the wave machine at a fierce 600 mph is only six inches deep. There's nowhere to hide.

In slow motion, I feel my pants ripped down to my knees and my own personal indoor water park is exposed to the horror and permanent scarring of all the prepubescent teens (who may have since written to me from their secluded monastery in France) lined up to surf.

Let me just report that I kept my cool, knowing there is

nothing, NOTHING one can do in this situation except try to make it as brief as possible. As I rolled up the wave to be deposited onto the "bank" at the top, I managed to yank my suit back up to the frugal position it originally occupied while rolling in such a manner that the poor afflicted youth were merely mooned and not faced with the full Monty. And let it be further known that I was man enough to make a joke about it then walk calmly down the stone steps back out into the water park.

Then I went right to my hotel room and locked myself in the closet.

PAUSEAHOLICS

I need to have an extravention. It's like an intervention, where one gathers the family together to solve an addiction. Except instead of them reading their sad, poorly punctuated letter to me, I will pull a crumpled paper from my pocket and read this heartfelt note: Your addiction to pausing the DVR has affected my life in the following ways . . .

Because my family IS addicted. They can't watch anything without a disproportionate level of pausing. They pause commercials. They pause movie credits. Yesterday, my son paused static. But they can't help themselves. They are afflicted with a terrible, terrible disease: I live with. . . PAUSEAHOLICS!

It's bad enough I'm being forced to watch the very dregs of television. My daughter makes me watch *Deadly Women*, my wife forces *Teen Mom 2* down my throat, and the boy inflicts the sheer hyperkinetic terror of *Adventure Time* on my sensitive palate. I can deal with bad TV—I grew up in the 70s, so trust me, I've watched at least one episode of *Love Boat*.

It's the pausing I can't take.

It takes my family three hours to watch *Hoarders*. They turn a thirty-second commercial into a ten-hour miniseries. I swear to God if they hit pause again, I'm going to throw the remote into the blender. My family members are pauseaholics. There is no cure.

It's not just the pausing that sends me into a conniption, it's the implications. If I walk into the living room, the girl will hit pause until I sit down. Now this might sound like a conscientious act, but the glare on her face and the white-knuckling of the remote tell a different story. I'm a giant intrusion, a Godzilla attack on the Tokyo of her televisonary experience.

The boy is worse. For him, *Supernatural* is not divided into episodes but into lessons on the occult. His constant pausing to Google the names of demons and the titles of musty old tomes turns a forty-four-minute glorified *Scooby Doo* into a Decalogue only an angry Russian ex-patriate philosopher could ever hope to finish.

My constant gasps of incredulity get me nowhere with these people. They are children of the future, and in the future, there is no such thing as continuity, and suspension of disbelief can be as fractured as the lives of the intolerable cretins they can't get enough of on *16 and Pregnant*, *Animal Hoarders*, and *I Used to Be Fat*.

I tried to institute a no-pause clause but was met with jeers of protest. My daughter actually played-paused-played as she explained, "You're [pause-play] so old [pause] you think paws [play-pause] only come on bears and [pause] dogs [play]." I tried to rattle off a snappy retort but she wouldn't give me the remote and just turned the volume up until I left the room.

It's insidious. We were driving to the store to get batteries for the remote, arguing about the fate of Egypt, when she tried to pause the radio to make a point. When it didn't work, she rolled her eyes as if the car was at fault for not coming with a pause button. It scares me because if she's my Star Trek future baby, then her every complaint about my antediluvian tech is an indication of what kind of head-swiveling technology I'll be trying to figure out when I'm old. I cannot imagine the incalculable death stats that will rack up when they can finally pause radio.

I'll just drive directly off a cliff and save myself the aggravation—although I'm sure, halfway down, the girl will pause me mid-air to ask me to get her a Coke on the way home.

FEEDING TIME IS ALL THE TIME

And so here I stand, hip deep in spent pizza boxes, McDonald's wrappers, and Popsicle sticks. My kitchen is piled to the eaves with sauce splattered pots, greasy pans, dirty dishes, and those plastic wrappers from Kraft "cheese" slices. I'm exhausted. I'm worn out. There's not a scrap of food in the house. I wipe the sweat off my brow, wipe my hand on my apron, and my phone vibrates. It's the boy, texting me from his lair.

"Food."

It's been like this for six weeks. He wakes up, eats everything, then asks me what's for lunch. I'm trying to keep ahead of him but it's hard. I hurry back into the kitchen. I make him a couple of sandwiches, some mac & "cheese," round it out with a pickle, a glass of milk. I come into his room, place the tray gently on the table in front of him so as not to disturb his run of headshots in DIE ZOMBIE DIE.

I break down the mountain of pots in the kitchen, chip dried gravy off the stove, and get everything back in order. He brings me the plate.

"That was good. What's for lunch?"

"I'm frying a horse."

"Dad, you're so funny. But seriously."

He eats like a Hobbit: breakfast, second breakfast, pre-lunch, lunch, post-lunch, second lunch—I think he eats in the shower.

And he's not getting fat. Not much. He's getting bigger. Like I'm zooming in. If his head and feet are any indication of how tall he's going to be (like 6'1" isn't good enough), I should start saving for a new ceiling.

And though most of the food is clearly being used as scaffolding to grow his new giant body, some of it goes through him the old-fashioned way and it's as much a problem coming out as it is going in.

"Dad, call a plumber."

"He was here five minutes ago!"

"Cool. What's for lunch?"

Yesterday he was eating a snack while looking in the fridge *for a snack*.

"You should go to the store. I need a snack."

"You're eating beef jerky right now."

He looks at the beef jerky in his hand.

"Well, it's almost gone."

I open the fridge. A starving village in Czechoslovakia stares back at me.

"I'm going to Wendy's."

"Get me a triple Baconator."

"Kid, you're too young for a heart attack."

"And a shake."

"Any last requests?"

"Hurry."

I hit the road. I reject my own principals. I drive through Wendy's. I bring home a heart attack in a box. I have one too. I feel dirty. I feel like I've crossed some kind of line. And I feel like I'll never eat again. My stomach is distended like I've swallowed a bowling ball. I walk in and three of his friends are there.

They've brought snacks.

They're eating on the couch like a pack of upright hyenas, the crunch of chips is deafening. They all see me and pounce off the couch, snatching the food from my carb stupor weakened grasp.

I've been gone fifteen minutes. There're six large empty bags of chips, beef jerky wrappers, and an eviscerated Combos bag. One of them has his head inside a sack of Funyuns. I could live a week on the crap they've eaten while I was out GETTING FOOD.

They tear open the fast food wrappers and growl.

"Thanks, Mr. G, we were starving."

MY STUPID CHILDHOOD

My childhood was a near death experience lasting about fourteen years and spanning three states. I was often only millimeters from being described with horrific phrases such as "over ninety percent of his body," "buried alive," and "he was such a quiet kid."

As part of the last generation to grow to teenhood sans Internet, I can confidently tell stories of what it's like to be outside without headgear and pads. I grew up mostly in swampland states (Alabama, Florida) and by the time I was ten I was at ease in the presence of snakes, alligators, escaped iguanas, wild boar, and vultures. By the time I was eleven, I'd burned down a forest, been chased by a wild boar, run naked and screaming through abandoned orange groves because I was convinced I was being chased by wolves, been poorly darted, accidentally shot at, and buried one friend alive.

I give you: My Stupid Childhood.

THE GREAT ORANGE GROVE MINIATURE CLIFFSIDE VILLAGE URINE FIRE DISASTER

A lot of people have, in the process of becoming my friend, had a moment where they felt the need to ask me, a man of leisure and refinement, why I had not used my obvious intelligence to make millions, end world hunger, or improve the World Wrestling Federation, and I always have to chuckle and tell them, "I wasn't always this smart."

Here's proof.

I grew up mostly in rural Florida, only a stone's throw from Walt Disney World, during the time when Central Florida was just beginning to boom. Old Floridians were selling off their land as fast as they could. Entire counties worth of orange groves were leveled, paved over, and subdivided into curbed, storm-drained, cookie-cutter neighborhoods with names as compelling and imaginative as Brook Glenn, Glenbrook, Brentwood, Glen Brent, Wood Glen, even Oakwood. Each one had a dramatic entrance flanked by swooping stucco buttresses with the name painted across in big loopy cursive.

The idyllic, pastoral fugue these names were supposed to invoke didn't affect the population much except when they were buying the home. I suspect my father got a glazed look in his eye when he looked at the brochure for Whistling Pines, never suspecting that as raging, bored, highly literate pre-teens, my friends and I would discover late one night the letters on our entrance were easily removed with a Phillips head screwdriver. He lived in Whistling Penis subdivision for fourteen hours before anyone noticed. If only we'd had YouTube then.

Without the narcotic effect of cable or video games, our minds were free and quickly turned to the detailed and somewhat destructive exploration of our new home.

As my pop was the plumbing super, we got a discount on a house. We visited it, from slab to roof beams, nearly every day, and moved into its gleaming vinyl interior in 1975. The subdivision had space for four hundred homes, only half were started. For the next three years, I lived in a construction site.

Which makes a lot of waste. Which has to go somewhere. Which is expensive. So to cut costs, they'd drive a bulldozer at a thirty-degree angle into the ground, making a long, sloping ditch. Over a year or so, they'd fill it up with trash, cover it with dirt, and build a house over it.

Of course, as ten-year-old kids, we didn't know anything about all that. All we know is one day we're taking a shortcut home from school. We stop at the bait shop and buy nickel cigars and we're smoking them in the dark shadows of the abandoned orange groves when we come to a huge hole in the ground.

It started at our toes and sloped gently down until the rim of the hole was several feet over our heads. You could see striated clay in the walls, citrus roots dangling like severed limbs, a little water seeping into the very bottom of it. And there was a tiny pile of trash way down there. We walked all the way in, amazed at the tufts of dill weed and long grass poking over the edge of it over our heads. And no one else knew about it. It was ours.

We immediately set out to create thrones. I found a big brass plate in the trash and used it to carve a hole out of the wall. My buddy, Tim McDonald, dug his out with a board and we stuffed ourselves into them. Then we used the trash to build a tiny village. We got into it, carving roads and garages and using twigs and pieces of cardboard from the trash pile to create huts and corrals and a ramp. Eventually, we had to step back and admire our work, a miniature primitive encampment a good yard wide, with several levels and connecting roads. It was a marvel of imagination.

Naturally, we had to set it on fire. And just as naturally, it only made sense that, in order to put out the fire (which was getting pretty big pretty fast), we would pee on it.

Now, if we had really thought about it, even in our wildest imagination, we would never have considered that in Florida, where it rains almost every day, where the tangle of weeds is so pregnant with moisture that even on a dry summer day in the afternoon if you walk across a field you'll be soaking wet—we would never have believed that trees might be dried out.

But apparently they were, as the orange tree that hung directly over our miniature inferno promptly burst into flames about the time we ran out of pee. We stood there in the bottom of this pit, horrified, as the next tree exploded, then the next, then—

We ran like hell. We dove between house rows and crept around garages and took another short cut through the little woods behind my house and snuck in through the sliding glass doors and were sitting in the living room watching TV when my dad burst into the house.

Sirens were wailing and smoke was drifting over the subdivision. Dad came in and told us half the orange grove just burned down. We acted rather astonished. Thirty years later I gave it up and told him, and he didn't believe me.

THE GREAT HYDRAULIC MUD-PACKED NEAR-DEATH TIME CAPSULE RESCUE DISASTER

There are times I look back on my childhood and wonder if I'm retarded.

It's possible. I mean, I could be just a highly capable retard. I make enough boneheaded mistakes now that I might just qualify. But for real evidence, you need to look back, back to 1975.

We lived in Whispering Pines subdivision, which was still mostly under construction. Every street had two or three homes filled with a family but the rest were open shells and in many cases, like next door to my house, there was just an overgrown lot.

These lots were the best. You could do anything you wanted to them. The dill weed grew well over our heads and, deep in the green guts of it, we'd find corn snakes, old bottles, discarded tools, and God knows what else.

For reasons that even deep hypnosis will not reveal, my buddy Tim and I decided we were going to bury a time capsule. Much like the NASA versions, ours was a Folgers can filled with some army men, our names, a couple of Hot Wheels cars, and loose change. We gleefully imagined the glory and TV time we'd get fifty years in the future when NASA dug it up and tracked us down and made us heroes.

We start digging. Now, the way we see it, a simple hole is just not enough. It's not dramatic. So we dig like champions, like miners, like only insane ten-year-old boys with visions of grandeur can dig. We shoot for China.

Near the end of the day, we had a beautiful hole with perfectly straight sides and a flat bottom and we were proud. Man, we were *proud*.

Only we couldn't find our can.

Obviously we'd covered it in dirt but we panicked, ran back into the house, turned everything over, forgot what we were doing, and ended up watching cartoons. Mom came in and saw the dirt all over our clothes and kicked us out. We saw the shovel in the middle of the driveway, remembered our mission, ran out into the field and beheld our magnificent hole.

It was awesome. Tim said, "Jeez, you could lay down in it!"

And he did. Dropped right down into it, comfortable as a warm tub. And without thinking about it, Tim yells, "Hey, man, BURY ME!"

So. I. Did.

I dove into it with all the gusto of our previous mission. I pummeled Tim's frail ten-year-old body with heavy dirt and pretty soon I had him covered.

You have to understand what kind of person Tim was. Tim was a highly intelligent manic genius. We'd already made an electric-powered lawn mower car, built an outdoor kitchen in the woods, a tree house with support poles that sprouted leaves, a hot air balloon toy, and wind-powered go karts. Of course, he was the evil genius (I'm the nice one) and many of our parts were, er, *procured through unofficial channels.*

We did set a lot of stuff on fire.

Through it all, Tim never stopped talking. Not only talking, but shouting and singing and planning and explaining. He was an incessant chattering drone and my childhood was underscored by his ceaseless speech.

In the hole, however, as the dirt piled up, Tim's demeanor changed. He got quiet. Studious. His permanent grin faded into a bemused half-smile. In the ensuing quiet I suddenly became conscious of my environment, of birdsong, of the wind through the trees, of . . . a kind of . . . quiet . . . gasping. I looked down and Tim was turning pale. He was having trouble breathing.

"Hey, man, this is NOT fun. Maybe you should . . . dig . . . me . . . out."

I suddenly realized that I'd actually buried Tim alive. He was buried right up to his neck in this hole and he was having trouble. Tim started to turn a little blue and hyperventilate. I freaked. I ceased to think in a straight line. I sought the counsel of my STUPID mind.

I often played in the yard with the hose. My parents called this watering the plants. I called it hydro-elliptical-maximum-distribution-studies period. During my studies, I had learned that the jet of water flowing from our hose easily penetrated the soft Floridian loam. Our water pressure was so high you could peel paint with it. I knew that I could turn it on high and easily ram it into the ground. I looked at Tim. I ran for the hose.

I turned it on full and drove it into the dirt over Tim's chest.

"WHAT ARE YOU DOING?!" he gasped.

"I'M SAVING YOUR LIFE!"

By now Tim's entire body had gone to sleep. As the hose dug itself through to Tim's skin—now incredibly sensitive—he screamed.

"YOU'RE CUTTING ME IN HALF!"

I screamed, "OH MY GOD I'M CUTTING YOU IN HALF!"

Tim was breathing shallow, losing color. Even his freckles were disappearing. And I was making mud. Not just mud: When exposed to the implacable sun for months on end, Florida's soil turns into a desiccated, thirsty powder. If you add water, you don' get *mud*.

You get *cement*.

Suddenly, my dad pulls up in his truck. He gets out and walks over grinning like always. His grin disappears when he sees what I'm doing, sees the panic in my eyes, sees the ring of blue around Tim's lips. He grabs the shovel and frantically, starts digging. I scream:

"YOU'LL CUT HIM IN HALF!"

Tim screams, "DON'T CUT ME IN HALF!"

My dad is yelling things I can't print here.

He dug Tim out, brushed him off, and sat in him the cab of his truck. Tim was slack and listless. I thought I'd killed him. Tim coughs hard for several seconds.

He looks at me and, with the kind of unhinged breathless enthusiasm only Tim could muster, says, "That was COOL!"

THE WIND-PROOFED BURNT-LEG POLYESTER ROCKET-POWERED MATCHBOX CAR DISASTER!

Childhood for me was an adventure involving snakes, setting things on fire, theft, smoking cigars, and innovative homemade toys of nefarious—and potentially lethal—design.

Every day, particularly in the summer, my friends and I were hustled out of our houses and left to our own devices. Given that we weren't anesthetized by cable, and we could read, and were bored, sub-genius eleven year olds, we tended to find ways to amuse ourselves that should've involved rope harnesses, fireproof suits, and an emergency unit on standby.

Take the rocket-powered car.

We learned about rockets pretty quick, and Tim McDonald's dad would happily drive us to the hobby shop to buy us rocketry equipment assuming it was keeping us out of street gangs and prison. Our chosen launchpad, our Cape Canaveral, was the swamp just west of the cemetery.

We built all kinds of rockets, launched them, and lost them. We'd launch during ceremonies, at night, during school. We didn't care. We just wanted to get as much stuff into the sky as possible.

Eventually, the intensive labor of building a rocket lost its appeal. The launch was the thing. The fire—that's all that mattered. We realized that there were plenty of rocket-shaped things lying around and immediately discarded our plans to build bigger and more aerodynamic rockets in favor of launching whatever was close by.

We launched Barbie dolls, GI Joes, picnic ketchup bottles, OWL brand metal cigar tubes—anything we could stick an engine into went up. Or around. Often directly back at us.

One day my buddy Mark English and I were forming a sidereal rocket launching cabal over a bowl of Fruit Loops and lack of cartoons. I had two C rocket engines but didn't have the launch rig. Mark had a nearly palpable, hyper insane need to be entertained, a book of matches, and not much else. We rooted around through the debris in his room and discovered a Matchbox car. Mark held it up with an evil glint in his eye.

We weren't scouts (yet) so *be prepared* wasn't part of our motto. Our motto was *Festina, prae mater videt!*[3] We raced out into the cul de sac, carved all the dry rocket fuel from the engine with a pocket knife, and piled it up on the ground. Mark rubber-banded the other engine to the car and pointed it down the street. We both assumed the positions of two preteen scientists, testing the wind direction with a wet finger, looking around for adults or cops, and hesitating for reasons that were entirely subconscious. (Our subconscious minds, mute with fear and indignation, couldn't actually tell us we were about to blow ourselves up, only make us pause meaningfully, which we took as some kind of noble gesture).

---

[3] Something like, "Quick, before Mom finds out!"

Mark knelt with a lit cigar to ignite the saltpeter and black powder pile and I did what came naturally back then, I listened to what the esteemed writer Neal Stephenson refers to as the *imp of the perverse*: I stood directly behind the engine, the car pointed away from me, and stated, nobly, assured, full of purpose and aplomb:

"You light it, I'll block the wind."

Mark set flame to powder. There was an enormous, powerful flash, the car leapt into the air, bounced off Mark's skull, slammed into the asphalt, then spun around for a minute or two before the chute charge blew. Then it just laid there, smoking.

Much. Like. My. Left. Leg.

I didn't feel any pain. I was wearing the usual assortment of 1975 clothing made entirely from petroleum, uncomfortable as a burlap sack, emblazoned with a motocross close-up. I was a flammable boy. My pants—long pants—were deep blue polyester with a smoking hole in the middle of the shin.

I pulled up my pants leg, and stared in horror as blackened skin peeled off my leg with them. There was a black oval about the size of a train-flattened nickel in the middle of my shin. The skin around it was bright red and there were pieces of melted polyester fused with charred Christopher, and things were curling up away from my skin like I'D BEEN HORRIBLY BURNED BY A ROCKET ENGINE!

We both screamed and ran away in different directions. I was literally hopping up and down while I ran. I was completely terrified that somehow this burn had morphed into an all-consuming holy fire and I was about to go POOF.

Tim McDonald's sister heard us and somehow collared Mark and found me limping home crying copiously, holding my charred polyester pant leg. She rushed us back to her bathroom (she was older than us, listened to David Bowie, and smoked—she was the epitome of wisdom), slapped some Vaseline on my burn, and smacked us both in the head for being, "such [DELETED] idiots!"

You might think we learned a lesson about improvising chemical fun, but I assure you we did not. We went on to ever more colorful ways of injuring ourselves, all predicated on the simple principal that a boy's untethered imagination, unlimited access to power tools, and depraved ingenuity add up to great stories told by people in slings, the worst case involving molten lead, a Coke bottle, and screaming. Coming soon.

THE DAD

The following articles aren't specifically about the boy, or the girl, or the horror, or my gay dog, Ty. They're about the baffling weirdness that is parenthood. They're about what your dad does when you're not looking. They're about being controlled mostly by your inner child who suffers from a head injury and slurs his words. They're about being helpless, being hopeless, and being human.

AIRPORT SANTA IS REAL

This is a true story.

Normally, wild exaggeration is part of my job description. But not now. I've been sitting on this story since my daughter was seven, and now I'm finally comfortable telling the embarrassing, ridonculous, stupid truth: *I believe in Santa Claus.*

We were headed out for the holidays. We were a young family, huddled together in the airport's waiting lounge listening to my inexhaustible daughter list her preferred Christmas presents for the eighty-eighth time, a list that extended to near infinity, and included live animals and living household items one can only purchase in a cartoon, when the big, white-bearded guy sitting behind us turned around and blew our mind.

It was Santa. Don't stop reading! I know—you've had it up to here with Xmas glurge. But this really happened. I swear.

My daughter's belief in Santa was as strong as my belief in gravity. Christmas was not a December event for her. Christmas was her life. She sang Christmas songs in June without a hint of irony and when this guy, this plaid-shirted, red-suspendered, bald, bearded, gnomish nut turned around, her heart stopped and, moments later, so did her mouth.

"That's a very long list," said Santa.

"Grhm Flurny Nerb," said Rah.

"It might fill up my entire sleigh," he winked. His eyes crinkled up with little Hollywood special-effects crow's feet. My daughter's heart restarted and she leapt into an embrace of this stranger followed by an interrogation about reindeer, elves, and the weather at the North Pole. My wife and I smiled warmly and basked in the crazy coincidence. We were starring in our own personal Christmas special. Other passengers leaned in to listen. They smiled and stole glances at each other to check their sudden and mysterious lack of cynicism.

I finally pried my daughter off the ironically dressed Canadian (I'm assuming—there was a lot of flannel) and she promptly fell into sugarplum dreams, drooling copiously on my wife. I looked at Santa.

"I bet you get that a lot."

"Well, I am Santa. So, yeah."

"Ha ha. Good one. So, uh, seriously."

"Chris, seriously. I'm Santa Claus."

As he said this, he pulled out his wallet. His driver's license read, "Chris S.C. Kringle."

And then my inner child exploded. I know, I know, he was listening before and heard my wife call my name and blah, blah, blah. You weren't there. It was December and there was snow and Dean Martin was singing *Silver Bells*. I'd just spent two weeks power-shopping, building a tree, falling off a ladder, and wearing plaid. I was sitting in an airport lounge with Santa Claus. Seriously.

I let loose. As my wife stared at me like I'd lost my very last struggling vestigial shred of sanity, I went wide-eyed, little-kid Mall Santa on this guy. My Christmas list unspooled. I practically sat on his lap. And he listened. He smiled. He asked questions ("A seven iron? Really?").

Ever classy, ever practical, my wife finally reached over and peeled me off of my seat. I tried to catch my breath and become an adult again.

And here's what still sticks in my barren, cynical, wasteland of a mind: He stood up, shook my hand, winked a randy Burl Ives wink at my wife, and walked away.

I got a seven iron (bought it myself—I'm not crazy) and my wife got a lovely diamond tennis bracelet. But after the tornado of torn of wrapping paper subsided and we'd put batteries into all the toys and had a cup of coffee, there was a moment in which my wife and I looked at each other and—for a moment, briefly—I think even she, the most practical woman in the world, was willing to believe we'd met an elf in an airport.

I still do.

HOW WILL YOU CELEBRATE INTERNATIONAL WATER DAY?

I remember when I cared for the little things. I remember when I photographed every flinch, every booger, everything my kids did. I remember when the fridge was so festooned with pictures of houses and suns and bunnies it looked like some weird Tibetan mountaintop shrine. And I remember videotaping. Everything.

I've lost those tapes. I honestly don't know where they are. Our house is perpetually in flux as vast flocks of underwear and bras migrate from the upper floors to basement and back again, and underneath it all somewhere is a box with enough footage of our kids to make a Scorsese movie. I was reminded of this, tonight, as I watched some dork with a camera glued to his face try to film his son make noises through a trombone.

I say make noises because even I, in all my glorious elaboration, cannot qualify the cacophony my son and all the other kids were creating with brass and plastic as music. It sounded like two coal trains beating each other to death with sousaphones.

My son was one of those trombonists. We're both into big band punk, and, yeah, it was great, I'm super proud of him.

Because he would shave the ears off the person in front of

him with his trombone, Roon has to play with the slide pointed at the floor, and my reward for rushing out into the killer Chicago rain was to just barely catch the crown of his head gently wobbling in the back row. And the guy with the camera.

This guy was into it, and as the kids plowed through *Old McDonald's Farm* with all the joy and verve of a condemned Russian prison orchestra, he was perfectly synchronized to the music. Mentally triangulating his position to maximize exposure of his neopreternatural child, yet minimize the amount of visual space his khaki-covered ass was ruining for the people in the front row, he pranced into and out of an invisible box as deftly as Marcel Marceau miming a cube. He's doing this through a series of tics and glances and pardon me's and I realize this is a dance of record all young parents do. We're like bees wiggling lines that point to the best flowers. It's not the digital record this guy needs as much as the dance that tells the rest of the hive that over there is a flower of rare and distinguished pollen, blowing sax.

I've been accused by camera wielding videophiles of not recording enough of my kids' lives. They ask, incredulously: Where are my tapes? Where are my DVDs? Where are my bushel loads of Polaroids and Kodak slick prints? Yeah, well, I don't have any, and the ones I do have are just weird. I didn't take a picture of Roon playing the trombone, but I once got a great shot of my girl's vanity in all its tangled, inglorious glory because ten years from now when she's talking up her neatnik newlywed husband about how she was a neat kid? Blackmail.

I never claimed to be a good photographer but I think I could probably take a good shot if I put my mind to it. And I know when a scene is worthy. But I don't want to experience my life through the objective lens of a MultiPixel Nikon. I like the patina ascribed to events by bad memory and the haze of prevarication. I like that the record of my life evolves as I tell it from humble vignettes into full-blown Vegas-level musicals with synchronized swimmers and trapeze artists. I don't like the truth. The truth is boring. Pictures, they're like corpses. But stories, they live.

Years from now, when I tell this pictureless story of Roon's recital I'll tell a version where he stands up in the middle of *Frère Jacques* to knock out a Tommy Dorsey number to a standing ovation; that Jesus appeared and gave Roon his own personal halo and recorded a promo for Roon's album on iTunes; that little second chair flute, Maggie Sween, turned around with tears in her eyes and kissed him right there and they're married to this day.

That beats the snot out of a picture any day.

TEACHING JUNIOR HOW TO DRIVE

Way back when, in each of my spawn's early days, back when they still wet themselves and ate mush, before they could cuss or say, "whatever—I'm checking it on Google," to any of my well-crafted tall tales, I taught them how to drive.

You may consider this somewhat irresponsible to which I'll say nyaah and, furthermore, nyaah, because you're probably a malicious tightwad who started your tough love program at the same time my kids were wielding a Chevy through Edgebrook[4] and you wouldn't know whimsy from a hole in the ground.

I think it's hard for grownups to grasp the magnificent and terrifying size of the world to a child. Which is kind of weird since every grownup started out as a kid. You'd think they'd remember. I guess the abrasion of height, puberty, and taxes eventually wears away the shine of childhood and we forget all about how the world used to be magical and wild. Some of us managed to recover a little of that shine, maybe through our iron grip on immaturity, a kind of Peter Panic, and we still find ourselves lost in reverie and imagination with the same force and totality as children. We remember how big the world is and having procreated, we wait for the moment when we can do something ridiculously cool to let them know we know. For me, I let them both drive.

[4] Edgebrook: A neighborhood on Chicago's Northwest side.

Cars feature big in the child mind. They've appropriated all the same connotations as horses in the dreamscape: freedom, power, conveyance, and a certain species of mysterious wildness. Letting a kid control that is ginormous. It galvanizes their bravado. I wasn't thinking about that when I popped them up on my lap, though. To me, it was just cool.

And it was a family thing. When I was their age, my dad put me on his lap and let me steer a Buick Skylark from our house to my grandma's, one abandoned field and three dirt roads to the south. Things were different then, he was smoking a Pall Mall and I don't even know if the car had any seat belts. I just know that Dad asked me if I wanted to drive, and I screamed, and suddenly my perspective changed. I was seeing the world from the headspace of a grup.

When my eyes rose so far above the rounded vinyl dash I was used to, I got a look at the world as grups see it. It really helped, mythos-wise, that we were in my hometown2, Ocoee, Florida, which is perched on the rim of a huge, perfectly round lake. We lived well up that rim in a crappy little rental on a red dirt road. My grandparents lived in a nicer home just a few dirt roads over. When dad popped me up on his lap, the Skylark was trundling along at the top of our hill and I looked down like a micro-Moses onto my house, my granddad's house, the houses of all my friends, all gathered together up above Starke Lake, which glittered like a mirror below us all, in a big dark green bowl of orange trees.

Dad leaned back and blew smoke out the window and I steered the idling car down the road and managed to make the turns and it was huge. Just HUGE.

I don't know how magical it was when I let the kids drive. Different times on the calendar but the same age for each kid, four years old. Same place: Edgebrook, same time: well after dark.

I popped Rah up on my lap and said, "You want to drive?" and she didn't even think about it. She grabbed the wheel and, not really getting it I think, tried to will the car forward. I dropped it down into D and we inched down the asphalt, all the way around the block, from her aunt's to her grandma's and back. She was flush with excitement and couldn't even speak when we were done. Roon was the same way. They both got out of the car and didn't say a word; they had their tongues stuck in their cheek trying not to grin. I think they experienced it as some kind of rite, it had a magical overtone, a spirituality they sensed and they didn't want their glee to break the mood.

They walked back into the house and plopped down in front of the TV, and as I strolled back into the kitchen to pick up a hand of rummy, I caught them, each of them, each time, glance over their shoulder to check me, to see if I was looking, to see if I was really that close to their world, and each time I kept myself from grinning, and each time, solemnly, fraternally, I winked at them.

LAUNDRY AS A FORM OF SELF DISCOVERY

Laundry sucks. In the two years I've been on house arrest, I've just now started to get the tiniest little purchase on Mt. Dirtyclothes, and that's just towels. I can keep up with towels. Everything else is chance.

Being the knight-like, selfless, humble servant I am to my family, I often reserve my own clothing to be washed last, which means, if I'm lucky, I'll get to it before Kohoutek shows up. However, I manage to get a shirt or a pair of pants clean enough to not run naked through Wal-Mart. Sometimes, I don't. Recently, I found myself wearing a T-shirt that had been on me so long it was taking phone calls and ordering lunch. I had to meet someone, pick up something at an office, and I figured I ought not look like I'd been abducted and dragged through a hayfield. So I put on the only clean clothing I could find: my Vegas suit.

You know the suit. I'm sure you have one too. For a guy, it's a bad-ass black suit with killer cufflinks, shoes like small Italian lapdogs lacquered to a fine black veneer, a white linen shirt with a thread count approaching infinite, and a tie that can only be compared with the "girl in the red dress" in *The Matrix*. Even my socks are cool. Fully Sinatra. The Vegas suit.

I drive to the appointment listening to, no kidding, Sinatra, and feeling pretty swank. I swagger into the office and the girl behind the desk smiles at me. She grins actually, a full on ear-to-ear, and I just assume she's digging the Vegas suit. So I stand there, hands in my pockets, swinging my tie, being cool. I'm Joey Bishop. I'm Dean Martin.

The girl is still grinning. She picks up her receiver and whispers something into it, and I scan the room and decide whether I'll pick up the *USA Today* or gaze coolly out the window when the grinning receptionist buzzes a friend through, another woman, who breezes into the room, takes in the Vegas suit, and lays a smile on me that makes me hear music. For a married man, this is a good day.

Another office worker walks through from the opposite door and grins at me and shares a look with the receptionist and I start to get a feeling, a kind of gnawing question, the idea that maybe it ain't my suit they're digging. That maybe a portly, middle-aged married man in a $400 suit is still not much different from Captain Kangaroo in black. I snap back into reality. Nobody over twenty-two smiles at portly, middle-aged men no matter how much they work out, unless they actually drop wads of money in their path like crumbs—and that's not even a smile. It's a precursor of rictus. Nobody over twenty-two—*unless their pants are unzipped*.

I spin around and do the "I-think-I-forgot-something-in-my-pocket—no-no-the-other pocket—SHIT!" check which delivers a positive, YES, YOUR ZIPPER IS DOWN, YOU REGARDLESS JACKASS! report.

See, I recently started wearing suspenders. This is NOT proof that I am an ancient old dork, but finally cool enough to take off my jacket and roll up my sleeves, which I do on the rare occasion, like during a really distressingly hard game of Boggle. I just figured it was time. I needed that 1940s detective sobriety in my appearance. It's part of growing up. Besides, my damn stomach kept rolling over my belt letting my pants slip down and I looked a little too bubbalistic. What I didn't think about is how we are creatures of habit. Whenever I buckled by belt, I zipped. It was like punctuation. My suspenders suspended that habit leaving me frozen in the middle of an office with my hatch open below decks.

If I had only kept the laundry up. I would've been standing there in a belted pair of shorts with a Hawaiian shirt and my zipper welded tight.

However, I manned up. In full view I casually closed the barn doors and picked up that *USA Today* I'd been considering and went about my business, horrified by the idea that I'd worn this suit six times already since I got the suspenders and people smile at me all the time. At how many fundraisers had I unwittingly been the main attraction? I'd given a very popular lecture recently in this very suit, with these very suspenders. Very popular. Lots of applause.

I AM HEROIC. PERIOD.

My daughter's friends were over the other day. My daughter's friends are all hyper-intelligent and busy as hell, just like my daughter. But, unlike her, they all have hero-quality dads who bend steel bars with their bare hands for a living and rescue babies from vats of molten lead and, most of all, go away during the day to return haggard and stoic and dead tired sometime after 5 p.m.

I, on the other hand, wrestle laundry to the basement and immerse myself in the minutiae of dishwasher load–planning and the use of "bluing" to make my whites whiter. I also make twisted knock-knock jokes and have a tendency to sing where I ought to mumble, and I have, somehow, become their hero.

I didn't mean to. And I say "somehow," but I'm being unnecessarily (and uncharacteristically) modest—I know exactly how I became their hero: I told them I chart my daughter's . . . um . . . I keep a record of, uh . . . I mark the calendar for. . .

I'm steadfastly aware of her punctuation.

This is not the lowest depth of my steady emasculation, by the way. That was surely sitting through a stuttering presentation of a Hugh Grant movie so insipidly British even Hugh Grant was rolling his eyes IN THE MOVIE HE WAS STARRING IN. It was a chick flick so flicking chicked I think I grew breasts while I was watching. But, such is marriage. I made

[My Attorney] sit through *Spawn* once so I owe her forever.

It is, however, a most unmasculine thing to do, to chart the, er, grammatical manifestation of your little princess. In fact, if you are a man, just turn the page. I'm embarrassed, ok? Chicks keep reading—I might need your advice.

It all started because [My Attorney] is pretty much too frikkin busy to pay attention to her own [red swarm]. One day she was working hard, staying up late after a fourteen-hour day deciphering antennae displacement graphs or something equally insanely technical. She was sleep deprived and focused with such unwavering intensity that she actually burned a hole through a deposition with her very eyes.

She said, "God I feel like crap. I feel bloated and woggly and irritable and..."

"You're getting your [red tide]."

"I just had my [monsoon wedding]!"

"Yeah, 27 days ago."

She'd been working so hard she'd actually lost her sense of time. I think if she didn't have a calendar on her Blackberry, she wouldn't know what day it was. So her [Mighty Mighty Bosstone] snuck up on her and smacked her across the head. I felt sorry for my little legal Lolita and decided to add her [Insane in the Membrane] to my automatic calendar and I've been charting it ever since. To the minute.

Well, being that busy, she never really explained to the teen that this is a regular occurrence, that it can be expected, that JEANS DAY on the calendar is not referring to a dress code. So, in for a dollar if you're in for a dime. The next time my daughter screamed, "PAD!" from the bathroom, I tossed a couple in (like grenades) and put her on my calendar too.

So there she is, hanging with her friends. Hanging is way too energetic to describe what they do. They flop. They flop over the chair. They flop down in front of the TV. They flop down the steps and flop into the car and flop out. They're virtually boneless. So they were all draped across the furniture expending less energy than most dead field mice, when I casually mentioned to Rah that I'd stocked the bathroom with [ammunition] and she might want to remember that since she was due for her [Orc Horde].

Her friends howled with approval and the Polish one screamed out, "YOU ARE MY HERO!"

So there you go. My ability to suppress my natural male tendency to fish and work on trucks in favor of ticking off the days until the women in my life are assaulted by their respective [mammy tsunamis] has elevated me to the level of hero. I can see myself now, standing tall, cast in bronze, a metallic cape forever blown behind me in chunky statuesque bravery, my brow pointed ever eastward, my countenance ever grim, ever focused—a fistful of tampons at my side.

THE WATERPIK NETI-POT LISTERINE DON'T-TRY-THIS-AT-HOME SINUS IRRIGATION DISASTER

I'm probably not sane. I haven't just come to this conclusion—it's been growing on me for years, a sneaky, furtive suspicion that *I ain't raht*. It worries me a little, not because I'm afraid of being crazy, but because I don't want to infect the children. On the other hand, maybe it's genetic.

Case in point: Do you believe I find the demonstration videos of neti pots:

1. Disgusting

2. Totally hilarious

3. Inspirational

If you picked number three, welcome to your favorite book.

I rarely try things I see on the Internet. I don't drop Mentos into Diet Coke. I don't drift my car. I don't cycle-sleep. But when I saw the neti pot, I had to give it shot. How could I avoid it? It hits all the ten-year-old entertainment points: boogers, semi-inappropriate irrigation, sticking something up your nose, and laughing hard enough to blow Coke through your nose while you're blowing salty water through your nose. Through your nose.

As soon as I saw the video, I ransacked the house looking for some device that could stand in for a neti pot—a teapot, a water bottle, a baby's nose cleaner—anything. But I had nothing.

Then I remembered my Waterpik.

If necessity is the mother of invention, YouTube is the mother of emergency rooms. I'd like to say I stared long and hard at the Waterpik before I gave in to the *imp of the perverse*, but I never lie. As soon as I saw the Waterpik, I shoved it up my nose and turned it on. Ok, there was a moment of practical modification—I removed the actual pik—not because I found it indelicate to nostrilize something I often stick into my mouth, but because I only wanted to squirt some water through my sinus canal, not drill a hole through my frontal lobe. And I did rinse the tank out. Once. In hindsight, there are some other practical points I might've added to my pre-hydro-encephalizing checklist. I might've:

- ☑ Considered that my sinuses were blocked.

- ☑ Turned the damn thing down from "Saw Through A Diamond" to "Gentle."

- ☑ Rinsed the tank THOROUGHLY given that I often fill it with straight Listerine.

- ☑ Used water that was WARM, not BOILING.

- ☑ Not. Frikken. Done. It.

But I don't blog for myself—I do it for you, dear readers, and to give up merely because there were risks, discomforts, or potential blindness would be cowardly. I pressed on. I pressed the blunted pik into my left nostril, tilted my head forty-five degrees to the right, flipped the switch, and blew the top of my skull off.

To say that the initial sensation was one of hot, sharp, piercing agony would be like saying a firecracker is a lot like a nuclear bomb. A jet of boiling, Listerine-infused water shot into my sinuses, was rebuffed by a mucous plug like a steel door, and proceeded to abrade the delicate lining of my cranium like a pressure-washer filled with bleach. I realized right away that this novel use of a Waterpik wasn't going as well as my last attempt and, flailing blindly, as water was shooting out of my nose and spraying all over the mirror, I managed to grab the electrical cord and disconnect.

Now, there are many reasonable people out there who now are saying to themselves, "well, surely he'll give up after that ridiculous stunt." You'd be wrong. Failure is not an option. It's more like a state of mind.

I rinse out the tank, turn down the pump, adjust the temperature, and try again. Where the trial run felt like I was being stabbed through the brain with a light saber, the second try felt like getting punched in the nose by a very angry, very accurate dwarf. Clearly I was getting somewhere. I checked the power and saw I'd not turned it down as far as I could. I tried again and finally reached an acceptable level where it felt *merely painful*, like when you're at the beach and you come up for air the fourth time you've been nailed and driven under and as soon as your head clears the surface you get punched in the face by a nine-foot wave that drives four hundred gallons of salty water into the upper reaches of your sinus cavity with the force of a nail bomb. Like that. Only less gentle.

Unlike in the popular neti-pot videos on YouTube, the water ran out of my nose like I'd left the garden hose on and, instead of a gentle cleansing, instead of feeling like all the stuff in my nasal caverns—sand, dog hair, chunks of discarded Maduro cigars, old furniture, and a 38 Chevy—was being sluiced out into the sink, I realized with growing fear that I was packing it all up into the furthest reaches of my skull where it would grow into some kind of mushrooming alien pod sack. And I knew with terrifying clarity that in a few days my head was going to explode.

And it hurt. Like hell. So I stopped. So, take it from me, the Waterpik is not a durable substitute for a neti pot. That's my public service announcement for the week. Never say I don't give you considered advice.

PUGILISM AND THE BLACK PARADE

Maybe it's part of getting old, but I can't seem to spot Volkswagen Beetles until it's too late. By too late, I mean my son has drilled me in the bicep with a Chuck Norris knuckle punch and I'm howling with pain and barely able to drive us through insane Chicago traffic to the next Volkswagen Beetle, which I will not see. Again.

In case you are just now walking out of a life in a cave, punch buggy is the emerging Olympic sport of sighting Volkswagen Beetles and then, upon said visual identification of said Beetle of Voklswagenistic origin, promptly beating the crap out of whomever you're sitting next to. This game is played in the car, while driving, so if that person is the driver, then they better be able to maneuver sans right hand because the moment the person riding shotgun sees a buggy–WHAM–dead right arm.

Roon is addicted to this stupid game, a game surely invented by ten-year-old brothers back in 1835 when they didn't have the Internet or cars or decent health care and, on more than one occasion, I am certain, some poor Swedish immigrant buried an extra son after a buggy punch incident went horribly wrong. I can see him now, Amish beard wagging in the afternoon sun, leaning against a hand-made shovel in his white shirt and stovepipe pants, wide-brimmed hat held grimly at his side, "Vell, he vas a goot bouy, and he is viff Gott now—punch buggy!

(slam!) ooh!—gott to digg another hole, yah."

The game and my son's violent enthusiasm for it are underscored by his new obsession with My Chemical Romance, a group that wears almost as much makeup as KISS and has almost the same weird marshal influence on its ravenous, zombified ten-year-old fan base. I have to admit, I think they're a good group. I can hear the guitar player pretty obviously ripping off Queen and I doff my hat (well, do-rag) to his ingenious and talented thievery. But the group revels in some kind of grave obsession with the color black and death imagery and are trying, I think, to single-handedly create a new genre combining emo, which is like a curse word for ten year olds, and Goth, which is a level of cool ten year olds peer hopefully toward and whisper about and pretend to disregard almost as much as they pretend not to notice girls. A genre I think might be called Gothmo, or Emoth.

I remember when I was young I wanted to be in the KISS army. We all wore Army fatigues and KISS T-shirts and threw our horns-of-Satan salutes in the air and prayed for the coming revolt to be a violent, sustained, bloodbath of Biblical scope during which our heroes would descend from a lightning-streaked thunderhead and join us as we decapitated disco dancing yuppies with our razor-edged, flying-v electric guitars.

My Chemical Romance inspires a similar, though wussed-out, semi-military response in its fans, although they're all vegetarians and pacifists so instead of the KISS army they're more like the Salvation Army, dancing, sort of. So I get the music thing but I never, ever, hit my dad. Evidence to this fact is that I can type with both hands.

Together, along with the inch and a quarter he gained since January and the ability to wear my shoes, punch buggy pugilism and the enthusiasm for the *Black Parade*[5] are turning my son into that thing that's older than a kid but not quite a tween yet, and I can see the hairy gawky teen poking out of him like he's wearing some kind of costume. Just the other day he was sitting on the couch and suddenly sniffed and said to the room, "God, my pits reek."

And it's not the gleefully vicious thrill he gets spotting one of those stupid cars and punching me in the arm to the glumjoy cascade of electric guitar from My Chemical Romance that's driving home the fact that I'm getting older and so is the mini-me. It's not even the fact that I miss the same antibiotic-chalk-yellow buggy that's parked in the same spot every damn day and take a hit for it because I'm getting older and so is it. It's this: When he hits me, it's not like a kid is hitting me, it's like some dude is hitting me. It kind of hurts and after two or three buggies, I got to tell him to lay off and I pretend it's because I think it's boring. But the truth is, my arm hurts.

---

[5] *The Black Parade*, by My Chemical Romance, the band that made your cousin get her hair cut that way.

ACKNOWLEDGMENTS

Many thanks to my family: [My Attorney], Rah, and Roon; my further family, both real and assumed: my Dad, Bull, and my mother, Rev. Elizabeth Sherrel; Michelle and Jay Sylestine, Jakan, Jaron, Raven, and Olivia; Herbert Whitfield; David Garlington; Frank Garlington; Susan, Murfeus, Patrick Greene, Carolyn Watson Teel, Marya Murphy, and Michael Camarata; Bill, Jeff, and Greg; David J. Haynes, Dan Brill, and all my brothers; my patient and steel-willed Chicago editor, the incomparable, Tamara O'Shaughnessy of *Chicago Parent*, and my New York editor, the ever supportive, Susan Weiss, of *NY Parenting*; my publisher, the remarkable Sharon Woodhouse, for again making a brave choice; and finally to my gay dog, Ty, all of whom are responsible for my sense of humor.

Christopher "Bull" Garlington is a syndicated humor columnist, whose work appears in various magazines, including *Chicago Parent* and *NY Parenting*. He is co-author of the popular foodie compendium, *The Beat Cop's Guide to Chicago Eats* (Lake Claremont Press). Garlington's features have appeared in newspapers and magazines across the nation since 1989. He is the writer behind the infamous parenting blog, *Death by Children*, and won the 2012 Silver from the Parenting Media Association for best humor column.